BIRGER GERHARDSSON

The Testing of God's Son

(MATT 4: 1—11 & PAR)

AN ANALYSIS OF AN EARLY CHRISTIAN MIDRASH

Διὰ τοῦτο πᾶς γραμματεὺς
μαθητευθεὶς τῇ βασιλείᾳ τῶν οὐρανῶν
ὅμοιός ἐστιν ἀνθρώπῳ οἰκοδεσπότῃ,
ὅστις ἐκβάλλει ἐκ τοῦ θησαυροῦ αὐτοῦ
καινὰ καὶ παλαιά.

(Matt 13: 52)

D1453631

WIPF & STOCK · Eugene, Oregon

Wipf and Stock Publishers
199 W 8th Ave, Suite 3
Eugene, OR 97401

The Testing of God's Son
(Matt. 4:1-11 & PAR)
By Gerhardsson, Birger
Copyright©1966 by Gerhardsson, Birger
ISBN 13: 978-1-60608-691-9
Publication date 5/1/2009
Previously published by CWK Gleerup, 1966

Translated from the author's manuscript by

the Rev. JOHN TOY

To Kerstin

Foreword

The analysis of the synoptic tradition of the temptations of Jesus which is here presented is one of a specifically genetic character. It is intended not only as a piece of exegesis but also as a contribution to the investigation of gospel origins. I am anxious however to guard against false generalisations. The synoptic material contains many *Gattungen*; one of these, one among many, can be designated *haggadic midrash*; the temptation narrative belongs to this Gattung. I have selected this tradition as the object of analysis with two facts in mind: (1) the temptation narrative has a very slight connection with history; a priori, its historical value is minimal; (2) as a consequence this narrative gives us unusually good opportunities for observing the mechanisms of the *"work with the Word of the Lord"* carried out by the early church; in it the ways in which the early Christian scribes thought and the ways in which they created their *logoi*—at least those of a certain type—lie open for dissection. The extent to which other elements in the gospel material belong to the same Gattung and have originated in the same manner can only be established by further investigations.

The present work can be read independently of my previous writings, even though I have here pursued further the lines of enquiry outlined in them (see especially *"Tradition and Transmission in Early Christianity"*, 1964, pp 5—10, 25 f, 37—47).

The study *"The Testing of God's Son"* comprises eleven chapters. The four chapters which constitute the first fascicle were completed on 31st March, 1963 (when they were submitted in connection with my application for the vacant chair of Exegetical Theology in the University of Lund). Owing to pressure of teaching and other work I have been unable to prepare the remaining chapters for the press and since I do not want to delay any longer making known my exegetical thesis, the contours of which are clear enough after the first four chapters, I have chosen the expedient of publishing my study in two fascicles.

Since the Table of Contents is not included in the first fascicle, I have briefly sketched the course of the analysis in the Introduction, p 17 f.

Lund, 1st July, 1966   The Author.

Introduction

A. *The purpose of this study*

According to all three versions of the synoptic tradition, Jesus of Nazareth, immediately prior to his public ministry in Galilee, was baptised by John the Baptist in the Jordan and then tempted by the devil in the wilderness. The Markan version covers the latter incident in three simple sentences: Jesus is tempted by Satan; is with the wild beasts; and is ministered to by angels. A more extended treatment is to be found in Matthew and Luke, where an argument, a kind of verbal duel, develops between the tempter and Jesus over the true understanding and application of God's will as it has been revealed in the Scriptures.

This unique narrative has a fascinating exegetical history; its graphic imagery and mythological symbolism have stimulated to the full the fantasy and imagination of its interpreters who have, at the same time, found in it some of the central themes of the Christian faith and the Christian concept of existence. The reader is referred to the sketch given in E. Fascher's "Jesus und der Satan" (1949)[1] and to the relatively exhaustive treatments of patristic exposition of this pericope recently published by K.-P. Köppen (1961)[2] and M. Steiner (1962)[3].

A pericope of this nature has so many aspects that it is impossible to consider them all in this study; we shall concentrate on two of the most important: i) the origin and development of the narrative in its three versions and ii) its meaning. In fact, the nature of the sources makes it imperative that these two questions be treated together in a study of this type, for they are closely inter-related.

Scholars have long discussed the relationship between the short narrative of Mark and the longer ones of Matthew and Luke. There seem to be three main possibilities:—
i) There is one tradition only. The question then is: is the short version

---

[1] Jesus und der Satan. Eine Studie zur Auslegung der Versuchungsgeschichte (Hall. Monogr. 11, 1949).
[2] Die Auslegung der Versuchungsgeschichte unter besonderer Berücksichtigung der Alten Kirche (BGBE 4, 1961).
[3] La tentation de Jésus dans l'interprétation patristique de Saint Justin à Origène (EB, 1962).

the original and the longer a scribal elaboration, or is the long one the original and the shorter an abbreviation?

ii) There are two different traditions. Mark relates in summary form an exuberant popular story; Matthew and Luke reproduce another narrative from scribal circles.

iii) The longer version is a conflation of two traditions; the brief mythological statement found in Mark has been combined with an already-existing dialogue of a scribal character; alternatively, a scribal temptation story from Q has been enriched by Matthew and Luke with elements from a shorter popular story in Mark.

Later in this study (Chap 6) we shall return to this problem, but some preliminary comments must be made here. In both accounts we find a tradition that Jesus was driven out into the wilderness immediately after his baptism and that he remained there forty days to be tempted by the devil. It seems unnecessarily complicated to suggest that there are here two quite different traditions; the only reasonable supposition is that we have two versions of one and the same tradition.[4] It also seems inescapable that the Markan version, brief to the point of obscurity, is a concentrated and abbreviated form of a longer narrative, which could have been less restrained and more popular in tone than the stylised accounts of Matthew and Luke, but clearly is the same story. The main reason for thus affirming that the shorter and the longer texts are versions of the same narrative is that both are based on the Book of Deuteronomy. To this we will return.

Our attention will be mainly directed to the longer version, for the short, cryptic phrases of the Markan pericope are not a suitable basis for a reasoned historical investigation. Insofar as the shorter version can be given a plausible *historical* exegesis, it must be with the help of the longer; on its own it is only an enigmatic fragment of an early, otherwise unknown, haggada about Jesus before the beginning of his public ministry.

A possible method of beginning our study of the longer narrative would be to attempt to discover the redactional alterations of Matthew and Luke by comparing their two texts and so reconstructing an "original form" of this story, which they both have taken from Q. This is the process used, for instance, by A. Meyer in his justly famed and pioneering work published in the *Blümnerfestschrift* (1914)[5].

---

[4] Cf. R. Schnackenburg, Der Sinn der Versuchung Jesu bei den Synoptikern, in Theol. Quart. 132 (1952), pp. (297—326) 300 ff.

[5] Die evangelischen Berichte über die Versuchung Christi, in Festgabe H. Blümner (1914), 434—468. See the introduction, p. 434 ff.

We however shall not employ this method. It does not seem the best procedure to reconstruct an original text, which can only be a hypothetical one, and then to make that the basis for an investigation: the element of uncertainty is brought in unnecessarily early. We shall analyse the three passages separately, preserved as they are in a copying tradition that is very satisfactory from the textual point of view. The Matthean version will be the basis of our study and we will devote only one chapter (Chap 6) to the accounts of Mark and Luke; most scholars regard the Matthean as nearer to the original than the Lukan[6] and to their arguments we will add a further one. We will show that it is in the Matthean version that we can still see how the temptation narrative was born and indeed, still perceive the cord joining the new-born babe to its mother. Our investigation will confirm the priority of the Matthean version in all essentials.

B. *The temptation narrative as midrash*

From a form-critical point of view the longer temptation narrative is to be placed in the category of *haggadic midrash*. The tempter bases his assertions on passages or themes from the Scriptures, and Jesus answers with scriptural quotations. The three decisive replies in the dialogue are all from Deut 6—8, the deuteronomic exposition of how God allowed his "son" Israel to wander for forty years in the desert that he might discipline and test him. The task before us therefore is to define more closely the relationship that indisputably exists between the account of how "God's son" Jesus was tempted in the desert in Matt 4:1 ff & par, and the account in Deut 6—8 of what God said to his "son" Israel in the desert.

A closer examination of the texts shows that the relationship cannot be plotted out merely by examining the actual quotations; a wider comparison must be made, embracing the themes of the dialogue and even the scenic background. The temptation narrative was not written by some simple soul who constructed his story with a few suitable quotations from an old and valued scroll: on the contrary, we have in it a narrative whose every detail bears the stamp of the late-Jewish (and early Christian) scribal tradition. It is an example of an early Christian midrash.

When we give our narrative such descriptive titles as midrash or haggada we are not doing anything new.[7] What we propose is to let

---

[6] Cf. A. Feuillet, Le récit lucanien de la tentation (Lc 4, 1—13), in Bibl. 40 (1959), pp. 613—631. See infra, Chap. 6.

these terms be more than mere form-critical labels designating one type of material out of many. By analysing the temptation narrative in the light of the laws which governed midrash exegesis and the development of haggada in late Judaism, we shall seek to *clarify and demonstrate its character of haggadic midrash*, investigating the raw material out of which it was constructed, and how it has been moulded into a unity, thereby elucidating its meaning. This is also a "paradigmatic" study; I am trying to demonstrate a method for "genetic" analysis of one particular type of gospel tradition.[8] The extent to which other parts of the gospels have the same character and originated in the same way can only be determined by further detailed study along these lines.

The author desires, at the outset of this study, to warn against drawing unjustified general conclusions from its results. The time is surely past when it could be claimed that all the elements in the gospel tradition originated in one and the same way; their history is much more complicated than that. The temptation narrative, for its part, belongs to the complex dealing with the period before Jesus' public ministry: that places it in a definite category. The framework of the narrative is more mythological in character than is usual in the synoptic traditions,[9] and the actual replies are unique in that Jesus speaks only in

---

[7] Principally Meyer, op. cit. This pioneering work suffers from a lack of understanding for the principles on which midrash was developed in Jewish tradition. The broad approach of the author, which follows the lines of the science of comparative religion, does not do justice to the particular metaphorical character of the Judeo-Christian tradition. Among works emphasising the Old Testament background of the narrative, see J. Dupont's stimulating study, L'arrière-fond biblique du recit des tentations de Jesus, in New Test. Stud. 3 (1956—57), pp. 287—304.

[8] This is my first attempt to elucidate the complicated question of gospel origins by analysing the existing traditional material, in accordance with the programme I outlined in the final chapter of my work, Memory and Manuscript. Oral Tradition and Written Transmission in Rabbinic Judaism and Early Christianity (ASNU 23, 1961), pp. 324—335. [In addition, see now my pamphlet Tradition and Transmission in Early Christianity (CNU 20, 1964), 47 pp.]

[9] The attempt to portray the temptation of Jesus as an historical episode in his life of the same kind as the other gospel episodes, requires a rather peculiar type of argument. See the dispassionate discussion in D. F. Strauss, Das Leben Jesu (4 ed. 1840), §§ 53—56. Cf. also Meyer's—somewhat ironic—account, op. cit., p. 437 ff. The philosophic background to the problem is exposed admirably by Fascher, op. cit. In my opinion it is essential to observe the dissimilarity between the accounts of what happened *while Jesus had his disciples about him*, and those that concern the period *before Jesus' public ministry*. It is an indication of the vital role played by the disciples as the sources of information. Exceptions to this cannot be discussed here.—Cf. Memory, p. 182 ff.

the words of Scripture. One cannot generalize about gospel origins from results obtained from material such as this; before such generalisations can be made, the remaining material, or at any rate representative selections from all its different "Gattungen", must be carefully analysed by a similar process.

Nevertheless the author does not want to minimize the implications of his results. The temptation narrative reveals much about the didactic activity of the early church; it is an unusually clear example of the work of a qualified scribal expositor. In another study, we have maintained that there was in early Christendom a special "work with the Word of God".[10] The nature, or varying natures, of this "work" can be more precisely defined only by a comprehensive analysis of all the types of gospel material. The temptation narrative *proves* that there was such a work with the Word of God in the early church, even though it exemplifies but one form or category of it. The very existence of this tradition however compels us to take up a whole series of new inquiries and to look again at a number of old ones. See later, Chap 11.

C. *The making of midrash*

All the varieties of late Jewish piety known to us are distinguished, despite many shades and nuances, by one characteristic: they are *torah-centric;* they acknowledge the Torah as the authoritative teaching given by God to His chosen people.[11] This sacred teaching has the character of *tradition;* it, or at any rate its kernel, is derived from the authoritative fathers. As a tradition, it is not static, merely being reproduced from one generation to the next. It is like a living stream, and new truths and insights can emerge from it without the old being disregarded.

At the beginning of the period with which we are concerned the Law (Pentateuch), the Prophets, and to a large extent even the other Writings, had for some time been established as the Scriptures, forming the basic part of the authoritative tradition. This did not mean however that there were no more variations or new forms, nor that the evolution of new themes and outlooks was checked. The Scriptures were enclosed in the compact and luxuriant atmosphere of a tradition of

---

[10] Memory, pp. 330—385. Cf. especially pp. 85—92, 101—112, 171—189, 234—261. [In addition, see my Tradition and Transmission, pp. 37—47.]

[11] There were differences of opinion among the various late Jewish groups about which teaching should be counted as Torah. For an introduction to terminology and fundamental concepts, see Memory, pp. 19—32, 71—84.

embellishment and interpretation—the targum and midrash tradition. The texts could be read out of the scroll and imprinted on the memory without much change taking place; but in the translation and exposition, renewal and growth crept in—new fresh leaves were blown in among the old.[12]

The growth of midrash—and in what follows we only speak of the haggadic midrash—is a complicated and varying process which we shall not attempt to describe in detail; the proper scientific study of it is still in its infancy.[13] In general terms we could say that the phenomenon is one of new and fresh ideas emerging from within a conservative traditionalism. Midrash is normally composed out of already-existing material, accepted as authoritative because it comes from the Scripture or the tradition. Using this raw material, the new is evolved. Naturally new terms, new phrases, new symbols and new ideas are introduced but the greater part is taken from that which already exists in the authoritative tradition. Midrash starts from a (sacred) text, a phrase or often a single word; but this text is not simply explained—its meaning is extended and its implications drawn out with the help of every possible association of ideas.

When the expositor is a scribe, the associations are primarily with other passages of the Bible; those similar in form or content are combined and conflated even though sometimes the connection between them is extremely tenuous. The possibility of vocalising the unpointed Hebrew text—i.e. the individual words—in different ways greatly extends the scope for fanciful and far-fetched exegesis.[14]

The memory of a scribe however is not simply loaded with scriptural texts which have been learned by heart: it retains also remembered sayings from the whole complex of authoritative exegetical tradition, which are employed in a similar manner to the Scriptural quotations.[15] It is most instructive to see how a characteristic terminology develops within the different exegetical schools; there is a whole treasury of phrases and images which is drawn upon even when the newer traditions are emerging.[16]

---

[12] Cf. op. cit., pp. 67—70, 79—84.

[13] For an excellent account of the present state of research, see G. Vermes, Scripture and Tradition in Judaism. Haggadic Studies (Stud. Post-Bibl. IV, 1961), introduction, with literature.

[14] Memory, p. 19 ff., with literature.

[15] See Memory, pp. 71—189, for a discussion of how the mechanical methods of studying affected the formation, use and transmission of the tradition.

[16] The different technical terms and slogans used by the various schools in their "work with the Word of God" have been usefully classified and interpreted by

Using this inherited authoritative and sacred raw material the scribes composed the midrashes; new puns, parables and narratives were created to pass on the boundless wisdom of the Torah to the listeners in new forms. The characteristic feature was the abundance of associations it contained, and the manifold use made of the well-known imagery of Scripture and tradition. It is probable that much of the persuasive power of a midrash saying lay in its associations with striking and beloved passages from the Scriptures and the traditional expositors.

The indications of this complicated and diversified phenomenon in the *Geistesgeschichte* given here must suffice. It needs to be added that the haggadic midrashes must not be treated as if they were all of one and the same type. The late Jewish haggada was so varied in its content, ranging from the most sacred and innermost thoughts of the Divine mind down to the most trivial things of the world's day-to-day life. The haggadic midrashes have emerged from different contexts; the expositors themselves belong to different ages and milieu, they have had different personal presuppositions, they have been guided by different motifs and questions, they have worked for different purposes. For this reason the sketch we have given above ought not to be concluded without an admission that a certain amount of simplification has been necessary.

Finally another problem must be briefly dealt with—the relation between the contribution made by the individual rabbi and by the scribal *collegium*, a very complicated matter. Each rabbi had a deep loyalty to the sacred tradition which he had received from others, and this set certain bounds to his originality and creativity. Much of his teaching also was given in communal discussions with colleagues and pupils and in this way his personal contribution was influenced by the corporate mind. Nevertheless the originality and creative achievements of the mature teacher must not be undervalued. The sayings attributed to one of the famous rabbis when collected together from the various rabbinic sources show that the inventiveness and imagination of the individual teacher has not been erased by the corporate "work with the Word of God".[17] We must not then ignore the significant role play-

numerous scholars, above all by "der Altmeister" W. Bacher (Die exegetische Terminologie der jüdischen Traditionsliteratur 1—2, 1889—1905). Nevertheless the metaphorical language of the haggadas of the various schools still requires scientific study, although an important beginning has been made by Vermes in his work mentioned above. The kind of analysis we are here prosecuting with regard to the gospel temptation narrative needs also to be done with the actual Jewish midrash material. Vast fields lie open here for research.

[17] See W. Bacher's classical works on the various tannaitic and amoraic teachers and the material assigned to them in the rabbinic tradition.

ed in the development and renewal of tradition by the leading, mature and authoritative rabbis as *individuals*.

In the following pages we shall designate the one who created the early Christian pericope about the temptation, the *narrator*. Although the narrative seems to be the work of one man, this does not imply that we regard him as an isolated "author" for in all probability he was active within a circle (school, community). Moreover with the passage of time his work could have undergone some changes; details could have been altered in the course of its use in the teaching of the early church, before the synoptic gospels received their final form.

D. *The Old Testament in the perspective of late Jewish period*

In this study we shall devote much attention to ideas and texts from the Old Testament; some comment is required on the method to be employed. The task before us is to clarify and demonstrate how a midrash arose in the church during the first century A. D. We shall try to show that the raw material for this was found partly in the Old Testament texts and partly in late Jewish and early Christian tradition. We do not need to examine the origins and development of the themes in the period before the Old Testament received its final form; what will interest us is the situation at the beginning of the Christian era, for at this time that which is primary and that which is secondary exist *side by side* both in the Scriptures and in the tradition; the secondary often having more relevance and vitality than the primary. (This was the case, for example, with the term "Son of God" which, though in origin probably a royal epithet, was at the beginning of our period, according to the sources, more frequently used of the people of God than of the "Anointed One".[18]) We must give facts of this kind their due weight if we are to describe clearly and accurately the situation in the time and milieu which concerns us. It will also be necessary to point out how certain themes in the Old Testament began to be seen in a new light and how new interpretations were given of them, in the inter-testamental period.

A comment must be made concerning the divine name, Jahve; it is necessary to use this name in presenting our material since, in certain contexts, it has a special, distinguishing function which the general term "God" does not have. Yet on the other hand, to do so strikes a discordant note, for this was the name which was too sacred for the

---

[18] See infra, Chap. 1 B.

Jews of that time to dare to pronounce. So as not to conflict too sharply with the values and ethos of our period, we have chosen to reproduce the name only in its consonantal form, JHWH.

E. *The course of the analysis*

As already stated, and as we shall proceed to demonstrate, the temptation narrative is an early Christian midrash, based on a text from the Old Testament, as this was interpreted in the late Jewish period. The present task is to place the origin of the narrative in its historical context. Just as the origin of the early church must be seen against the background of its period, so also must the development of the early Christian midrash be seen in the light of its late Jewish setting. Tracing the history of ideas in this case is not without its difficulties. Within the framework of one living tradition we have to trace the beginning of another. Two extremes must be avoided: the originality of the new tradition must not be predetermined so that insufficient weight is given to the historical sources; nor, on the other hand, must the true originality of the new tradition be undervalued because of its general affinity to other contemporary material. In the former case justice has not been done to the "genus proximum", in the latter to the "differentia specifica".

Our plan is as follows: we shall define the relevant raw material at the disposal of the early church and determine step by step how this material was used and what new values and implications the account receives from its early Christian setting.

In the first two chapters we take the two main themes of the narrative—Son of God and temptation—and examine them in their late Jewish context. In the next chapter (3) we shall analyse all the details of the narrative in the light of the contents of Deuteronomy 6—8 as this was understood in the late Jewish period. In the fourth chapter we shall seek for the basic idea which unites the three temptations to each other and to Deuteronomy. In the fifth chapter we shall place the preliminary interpretation, so far attained, beside the teaching of Jesus to see how it is related to it: to what extent it is in agreement with it and influenced by it. In Chapter 6 we shall examine the variants in Mark and Luke, not simply for their own sake, but also to see if they contribute to the solution of our two main problems. The next chapter (7) is devoted to the context of the Matthean account; in the first place we shall examine the significance of the connection with the narrative of Jesus' baptism, in the second the place of the story in the gospel as a whole. Then, in Chapter 8, we can set the temptation pericope in relation to the idea of the "Son of God" as we meet it in the rest of the New Testament, in both its Christological sense and in its plural form "children of God". Chapter 9 is devoted to the ideas of "temptation" in the rest of the New Testament and to the relations of our narrative to them. With this the investigation into the meaning of the story is concluded, but two further questions still need to be answered, the point of time when the narrative emerged and its original language; these are dealt with in Chapter 10. The final chapter summarises the results and points out a number of new problems arising from this study. Two problems require treatment in Excursuses: the question of the relation between JHWH and his angel in the exodus and wilderness traditions, and the complicated question of earthly and heavenly bread.

CHAPTER ONE

The Son of God

A. *The key term in the temptation narrative*

In all three accounts, the temptation of Jesus is clearly related to his baptism. As Jesus steps up from the waters of the Jordan, the *Spirit of God* descends upon him and a heavenly voice pronounces him *"Son of God"*. Then he is led by *the Spirit* into the wilderness there to undergo the temptations, two of which begin with the words "If you are *the Son of God* ..." It cannot be more clearly indicated that both accounts belong together, not merely by a loose conjunction, but because they share the same principal theme.[1]

This is the case in all three versions. Luke[2] certainly inserts the genealogy between the accounts of the baptism and the temptation (3:23—38) but he refers back to the baptism account with the phrase *"full of the Holy Spirit* Jesus returned from the Jordan and was *led by the Spirit* for forty days in the wilderness" (4:1).

At a later stage we shall investigate this connection more closely and see what conclusions can be drawn from it (Chap 7); the fact of the connection is all that here needs to be pointed out and emphasised: the narrative is about the temptation of the *"Son of God"*. The principal term is "Son of God", υἱὸς τοῦ θεοῦ.

Exegetes of the temptation passages have long debated whether or not the three temptations are "messianic"; the question of course is relevant, and we shall return to it later in Chapter 8, but it can distort the discussion and lead to inadequate exegesis. The intensive investigations of recent times into the messianic ideas of late Judaism have established that the various "messianic" titles cannot simply be equated, and the various ideas cannot be built into one unified system. In spite of similarities and affinity, they have different associations and implications. We need only to remind ourselves of the fact that accord-

---

[1] The connection has often been pointed out. See e.g. Schnackenburg, Der Sinn, p. 301, G. H. P. Thompson, Called-Proved-Obedient, in Journ. of Theol. Stud. 11 (1960), p. 9, and E. Lövestam, Son and Saviour (CN 18, 1961), p. 98 f.
[2] Cf. Schnackenburg, ibid.

ing to the synoptic tradition, Jesus cannot use the title "Messiah" of himself but can employ such terms as "Son of Man".[3]

It is most important therefore in detailed exegesis to pay special attention to whichever Christological title is being used, and to the associations and implications that it bears—although this does not mean that one loses sight of the common bond between them, the one theme to which they all give expression.

In the temptation pericope the term "Son of God" is used and not the terms "Messiah" or "Son of Man". As we shall demonstrate, it is vital to hold this fact in mind. That which is to be put to the test is precisely Jesus' *sonship*: the term *Son of God* is *the key term* in the narrative.

B. *The idea "Son of God" in late Jewish thought*

The temptation narrative is openly and unmistakably linked to Deuteronomy 6—8 at its three decisive points; the three answers of Jesus are direct quotations from these chapters. The principles which determine the attitude of the Son of God at the moment of temptation are taken from Deut 6—8. With this as our starting-point we must now examine this relationship more closely.

These chapters must not be isolated from the rest of the book, with which they share the same themes and phrases. Nor must Deuteronomy be separated from other Old Testament passages concerning the wandering in the wilderness. For example, the Book of Deuteronomy itself is a type of midrash or homiletic rewriting of the four more ancient books of the Pentateuch[4] and so it must be studied in that context. Furthermore, the treatment of the desert wandering in the other parts of the Old Testament show us the themes, phrases and images

---

[3] The reasons in favour of Jesus' use of the term Son of Man of himself during his public ministry are convincing. See (against Bultmann and many with him) R. H. Fuller, The Mission and Achievement of Jesus (1954), pp. 95—108, and O. Cullmann, Die Christologie des N. T:s (1957), pp. 154—167.—H. Riesenfeld (Le caractère messianique de la tentation au désert, in La venue du Messie, Rech. Bibl. VI, 1962, p. 53 f.) maintains that the term Son of Man is used principally in the gospel tradition to emphasise his apostleship visavi his fellow men whereas the term Son of God is used to set Jesus' saving work in the context of the whole salvation history and the execution of God's sovereign will.

[4] On the literary character of Deuteronomy see M. Noth, Ueberlieferungsgeschichtliche Studien 1 (1943), pp. 87—110, G. E. Wright, The Book of Deuteronomy, in The Interpreter's Bible 2 (1953), pp. 309—537, and G. von Rad's general article, Ancient Word and Living Word, in Interpretation 15:1 (1961), pp. 3—13.

that were normally used in describing it. It is essential to bear in mind the principle, generally applied throughout Jewish scribal circles, that biblical texts dealing with the same theme or having characteristic formal similarities, were brought in to interpret each other. As we have already observed, material could come not only from the Scriptures but also from the exegetical tradition. We must therefore try to reconstruct the material available to a first century scribe as he read passages such as Deut 6—8.

The theme "Son of God" was deeply rooted in the traditional religious ideology of Israel. It was a favourite variant of the election and covenant themes and indeed in the late Jewish period these three were virtually inseparable; for many centuries Israel had been accustomed to thinking of herself as a chosen people, and as God's covenant people and as God's son.[5]

These elements in the Jewish people's understanding of themselves were particularly linked to the texts and traditions of their early history: the miraculous delivery from Egypt, the wandering in the wilderness and the covenant-making at Sinai. In these early events—as in the lives of the patriarchs—it could be seen how JHWH "created" his people, "gave birth" to them or, as it could also be expressed, how he "found" and "chose" them: how he became Israel's "father" and how the people of Israel became his "son".

We do not need to discuss here the characteristics of this fatherhood; we proceed instead to enumerate a number of the most important *concepts* and *formulations* to be found in the texts dealing with God's son.[6]

The most significant text is the words of JHWH to Moses in Exodus 4:22 f where Israel is pronounced for the first time to be the son of God "And you shall say to Pharaoh,' ... Israel is my first-born son (בני בכרי) ... Let my son (את בני) go that he may serve me.' "

The prophets also speak of Israel as the first-born son of God: in Jeremiah 31:9, for example, the title refers to God's choice of Israel in ancient time "for I am a father to Israel, and Ephraim is my first-born".

The election-love of God is strongly emphasised. It is well known

---

[5] For an attempt to analyse these different themes as they appear *in the O.T.*, see H. Wildberger, Jahwes Eigentumsvolk (ATANT 37, 1960).

[6] On the O. T. concept of Israel as God's Son see J. Bieneck, Sohn Gottes als Christusbezeichnung der Synoptiker (ATANT 21, 1951), pp. 12—26, P. A. H. de Boer, De Zoon van God in het O. T. (1958), as well as the works named infra in notes 7 and 8.

that the Hebrew term אהב, "love", often means the same as בחר, "choose". Israel is the beloved son of God. A well-known oracle of Hosea says, "When Israel was a child I loved him and out of Egypt I called my son" (11:1). Jer 31:2 f speaks of JHWH's "everlasting" love for Israel and Deut 7:6 ff tells how God chose Israel for his own possession not because of Israel's merits but because he loved this people. JHWH's election-love for Israel is also mentioned elsewhere in Deuteronomy (see 4:37, 10:15 etc).

The theme of God's paternal relationship to Israel receives vivid treatment in the passages dealing with the wandering in the wilderness. Hosea reminds Israel-Ephraim of what God did for the people when he called his son out of Egypt "it was I who taught Ephraim to walk, I took them up in my arms" (11:3). Deut 1:31 speaks of JHWH bearing Israel through the desert "as a man bears his son" and in Deut 8:2 ff God lets the Israelites wander in the desert for forty years to humble and test them and to discipline them "as a man disciplines his son". We shall deal with these themes more thoroughly later in our investigation (Chap 3 C b); we mention them here to show that *many concrete and powerful expressions of the Son of God idea are to be found in the desert wandering texts, not least in Deuteronomy.*[7]

The sacred texts not only spoke of Israel as God's son, or, secondarily of the Israelites as God's sons; they contained also ancient formulae according to which "JHWH's anointed", the king (המשיח), was the object of God's love, the chosen one with whom God had made a covenant and to whom he had become a father—and so, in these passages, it is the king who is more properly "the Son of God": "I will be his father and he shall be my son" says the oracle on Solomon, the Davidic crown prince, 2 Samuel 7:14; cf Ps 89:27. Psalm 2:7 contains JHWH's promise to his anointed "You are my son, today I have begotten you" (cf Ps 110:3, LXX reading). Modern scholarship has maintained with good reason that these themes (Son of God, election, covenant etc) are part of a formalised complex of imagery referring originally to the king. When this imagery is used of the people it is a question of "democratizing" the originally royal epithets.[8] Be that as it may, in late Jewish times both the idea of Israel as God's son and that of the Anoint-

---

[7] On the Son of God theme in Deut (1:31; 8:5; 14:1; 32:5, 6, 18, 19, 20) see also P. Winter, Der Begriff "Söhne Gottes" im Moselied Dtn 32, 1—43, in Zeitschr. f.d. Alttest. Wiss. 67 (1955), pp. 40—48.

[8] See esp. I. Engnell's articles Förbund, Guds Son, Konung, Messias and Utvald in Sv. Bibl. Uppslagsv. 1—2 (2 uppl. 1962—63), and G. W. Ahlström, Psalm 89. Eine Liturgie aus dem Ritual des leidenden Königs (1959, with literature).

ed One as God's son existed side by side in the sacred texts. We must take notice of both these variants, but since the title "Son of God" in the temptation narrative is unmistakably determined by its use in Deuteronomy, it is the reference to Israel that demands our main attention.

In the Law, the Prophets, and the Writings, the texts which in late Jewish times were considered sacred and of inestimable worth, which were diligently studied and habitually used in worship and in teaching, the "Son of God" theme is to be found applied both to the "Anointed One" and to "God's people". If we turn now to the texts which *originated* in the late Jewish period we find that most of the material shows how alive and strong was the idea of Israel as "God's Son" at that time. This has been demonstrated in a number of accessible works to which we refer.[9] It is true that some scholars have denied that the other equation was made in late Jewish times;[10] certainly the evidence for the Anointed One being designated God's son is not so clear, some texts such as 1 Hen 105:2 and 4 Esd 7:28 f; 13:32, 37, 52, and 14:9 failing on text-critical grounds;[11] but other indications remain and new ones have come to light. The fact that in the sacred texts the "Anointed One" (משיח יהוה) is called Son of God, ensured that the original connection between the titles "Messiah" and "Son of God" was preserved. In the rabbinic literature we can see how the formulation of the scriptural texts conserved ideas which tended, for various reasons, to be neglected or unemphasised in the day-to-day instruction. 2 Samuel chap 7 will have played its part in keeping alive the identification between the Messiah and the Son of God. The recently discovered Florilegium Fragment from Qumran (4 Q Flor) presents us with a piece of evidence which is not surprising but very welcome:[12] in it the prophecy of Na-

---

[9] See S. Schechter, Some Aspects of Rabbinic Theology (1909), pp. 21—64, G. F. Moore, Judaism 2 (1927), pp. 201—11, H. L. Strack—P. Billerbeck, Kommentar zum N. T. aus Talmud und Midrasch 1 (1922), pp. 219 f., 392—396 and 3 (1926), pp. 15—19; these particularly on the rabbinic point of view. On the Son of God theme in the apocryphal literature, see R. Marcus, Law in the Apocrypha (Columbia Univ. Orient. Stud., vol. 26, 1927), pp. 6—16, and G. Ziener, Die Theologische Begriffssprache im Buche der Weisheit (BBB 11, 1956), pp. 47 f., 75—97. On the Son of God theme in the Qumran writings, see the literature cited in Lövestam, op. cit., p. 89 f.

[10] See the review of research in B. M. F. van Iersel, "Der Sohn" in den synoptischen Jesusworten (Nov. Test., Suppl. 3, 1961), p. 3 ff.

[11] See Lövestam, Son and Saviour, p. 88.

[12] See Y. Yadin's edition, A Midrash on 2 Sam. vii and Ps i—ii (4 Q Florilegium), in Isr. Explor. Journ. 9 (1959), pp. 95—98.

than is interpreted messianically, giving us an explicit statement that the Messiah is called "Son of God".[13]

It is nevertheless true that this application of the title is not *common* in late Judaism and that more usually it was a designation for Israel itself.

Chapter 7 which considers the connection between the baptism and the temptation narratives, and Chapter 8, dealing with the Son of God Christology and the children of God ecclesiology of the early church, will provide opportunities for extending this discussion further.

---

[13] See further Lövestam, op. cit., p. 89 ff.—W. Grundmann (Sohn Gottes, in Zeitschr. f.d. Neutest. Wiss. 47, 1956, pp. 113—133) maintains that in the late Jewish period the title Son of God was especially associated with the *high-priestly* Messiah. See infra, Chap. 8.

CHAPTER TWO

Temptation

A. The term נסה (πειράζειν) as a covenant word

If "Son of God" is the most important term in the temptation narrative, "tempt" ranks second. This term too has an unmistakable connection with the Book of Deuteronomy and with the other passages dealing with the wilderness wandering. Jesus is driven out into the wilderness to be tempted as God's son during or after forty days (and forty nights). In Deut 8 it states that JHWH has led Israel in the wilderness for forty years to humble and test (נסה) the people (v 2) and to discipline it "as a man disciplines his son" (v 5). Our first question is therefore: what interpretation was given to the verb נִסָּה, which was always translated by πειράζειν in the LXX?[1] To answer this we must consider the Old Testament material in its entirety.

The verb נסה has a fairly definite meaning. It is often used in conjunction with words like בחן (δοκιμάζειν, [ἐξ-]ετάζειν), "to test by trial", "harden", or צרף (πυροῦν), "to test by fire", "purge",[2] although, in contrast to these verbs, it never in the Old Testament has an impersonal object.[3] An exception to this is when it has a verbal object and means "to try to do something" but the Old Testament examples of this are few and unimportant.[4] Otherwise the verb *always has a personal object.*[5] In one place only in the Old Testament is it used of two

---

[1] The special purpose of this study does not require us to deal with the terminology of temptation in all its aspects, e.g. the small divergencies between πειράω, πειράζω, and ἐκπειράζω etc. See H. Seesemann, art. πεῖρα κτλ., in Theol. Wörterb. z. N. T. 6 (1954—59), pp. 23—37. Cf. also J. H. Korn's well known work ΠΕΙΡΑΣΜΟΣ. Die Versuchung des Gläubigen in der griechischen Bibel (BWANT, 4. F., 20. H., 1937).

[2] See W. Grundmann, art. δόκιμος κτλ., and F. Lang, art. πυρόω, ibid. 2 (1933—35), pp. 258—264, and 6, pp. 948—950.

[3] Therefore (against A. Sommer, Der Begriff der Versuchung im A. T. und Judentum, diss. 1935, p. 7 ff.) the basic idea cannot be to test in the same way that one subjects *material* to a test of endurance.

[4] 1 Sam 17:39; Deut 4:34; 28:56; Judges 6:39; Eccles 2:1; 7:23.

[5] Therefore M. Greenberg's theory (נסה in Exodus 20, 20 and the Purpose of the Sinaitic Theophany, in Journ. of Bibl. Lit. 79, 1960, pp. 273—276) that the basic meaning is "to have experience of", "to be used to", or "to be familiar with" cannot be upheld, even though these meanings may *approximate* to the significance of the verb when it refers to the testing of persons.

people who do not stand in any close friendly or covenantal relationship to eachother—the Queen of Sheba who comes to ask riddles (testing questions) and so "test" Solomon, or rather, "obtain empirical knowledge" about him.[6] This can be compared with Daniel 1:12, 14 where the word means "carry out an experiment with" (three servants).[7] Otherwise the verb is used in purely religious language, and it designates two different aspects of one and the same relationship: the context is the relationship between God and his people and within this the verb is sometimes used positively of how God tests his people, and sometimes negatively of how the people test their God. Philologists who seek to define the precise meaning of נסה ought never to forget the fact that the word is normally used within the covenant relationship—interpreted in its widest sense to cover all covenants between God and his worshippers whether the latter are a nation, tribe, family or even an individual (patriarch or king).[8] In these contexts the word seems to imply primarily *a testing of the partner in the covenant to see whether he is keeping his side of the agreement*. Additional meanings have become attached to this fundamental one in the course of time.

It is important to note that JHWH is not said to test heathen people, but only his own, the people of his own possession. When the term is used of an individual, it is always a pious man, never an ungodly one. Conversely, when Israel is the subject of the verb, it is always JHWH and not the Baals who are tested.

The covenant means that JHWH will be the god of his covenant people, will be "near them", "in their midst", "with them" and will fulfil all the obligations that pertain to divinity; giving to his people all that belongs to the divine blessing (ברכה): life, health, power, food, fertility, riches, protection, victory etc (Ex 6:7, 19:3 ff, 29:49 ff, Lev 26:11 f, Deut 28:1—14, Ez 37:26 ff etc).[9]

The people's obligations are defined with such words as to fear and love God, to worship and honour him, to be faithful to him, to listen to his voice, and obey his word, to walk after his commandments, to live in his law etc. "Faith" is a vital element here; faith meaning to

---

[6] 1 Kings 10:1; 2 Chron 9:1.

[7] The significance of the word and its use in Ex 15:25 is disputed. Some scholars maintain that there is here a corruption of the text. On the problem see E. Nielsen, Shechem. A Traditio-Historical Investigation (1955), p. 118 ff.

[8] See J. Pedersen, Israel, Part 1—2 (2 Dan. ed. 1934), pp. 205—386. For a review of the discussion about the O. T. covenantal ideas see K. Baltzer, Das Bundesformular (WMANT, 4, 1960), pp. 11—18.

[9] On the meaning of covenant see Pedersen, op. cit. ibid., and on the meaning of blessing, pp. 140—164.

"treat JHWH as reliable" (האמין, πιστεύειν), to trust him, to believe that he will faithfully and lovingly keep his promises and honour his "obligations".[10] What is required of the people in general is also required of each member individually.

We have already mentioned that the Old Testament speaks not only of a covenant between JHWH and his people, but also of one between JHWH and his Anointed One (esp. David and his seed).[11] The reciprocal obligations are the same in both cases.

B. *God testing man*

When the Old Testament speaks of JHWH testing his covenant son, "tempting" him (נסה, πειράζειν), it means that God arranges a test to find out if his son is true to the covenant, is נאמן, πιστός. It is almost a formula that God tests "that he might know" (לדעת) whether his chosen one is true or not.[12]

The classic temptation narrative of the Old Testament is the testing of Abraham in Gen 22. In verse 1 f the scribes read that God tested Abraham with a command to sacrifice his only son; he obeys and JHWH breaks off the test with the words "now I know (ידעתי) that you fear God" (v 12). Abraham then receives the promise of abundant blessing "because you have obeyed my voice" (v 18).

In Ex 16:4 JHWH informs Moses of his decision to let bread rain down from heaven for the people, and that they are to gather enough for each day and not more, "that I may test them, whether they will walk in my law or not"; cf also Ex 20:20.

In Deut 8:2 it is said that JHWH has led Israel into the desert "that he might humble you and test you to know what was in your heart, whether you would keep his commandments or not".

In Deut 13:2 ff Israel is commanded not to listen to false prophets or dreamers, even if they perform signs and wonders; "(in this way) JHWH your God is testing you to know whether you love JHWH your God with all your heart and with all your soul".

In two places in Judges we find the same idea. JHWH tests Israel (that he may know) "whether they will take care to walk in the way

---

[10] See op. cit., pp. 268—271, and Part 3—4 (1934), pp. 417—419, A. Weiser, πιστεύω κτλ., B. Der at. liche Begriff, in Theol. Wörterb. z. N. T. 6, pp. 182—197, and E. Pfeiffer's lexical study Glauben im A. T., in Zeitschr. f.d. Alttest. Wiss. 71 (1959), pp. 151—164.

[11] See Ahlström, Psalm 89, pp. 47—56, with literature.

[12] Cf. Sommer, Der Begriff, p. 7 f.; cf. Seesemann, art. cit., p. 24 f.

of JHWH or not" (2:22) and "to know whether Israel would obey the commandments of JHWH, which he commanded their fathers by Moses" (3:4 ff, cf 3:1).

In 2 Chronicles JHWH tests his covenant son, king Hezekiah, "to know all that was in his heart" (32:31).

Finally, although the verb נסה does not occur in the Book of Job the subject of temptation is dealt with with such power and wealth of imagery that this work became very important for the future treatment of this theme. Satan has received permission from God to take away from righteous Job all that he had received from God. The test was to reveal whether Job would stand fast by his innocence, honesty and faith, or whether in such a situation he would reveal himself unrighteous by breaking out into curses against God.

Before we proceed to note the other implications which the temptation idea has incorporated, we must glance at what is meant by man testing God.

C. *Man testing God*

Just as it is regarded as fully consonant with God's sovereign rights within the covenant to test his son, so it is seen as a grave religious offence for man to test God.

It is quite easy to understand what the Old Testament means by testing God if we remember that this occurs within the covenant relationship. To test God is to examine him to see if he will keep his obligations, challenging him to demonstrate his fidelity to the conditions of the covenant. It is usually a query raised by the covenant son, a demand that God should show by a powerful work, by a "proof" (מסה) or "sign" (אות or מופת) that he really is the god of the people, is in their midst, is active as their saviour, protector and provider in accordance with his covenant promises. This action is condemned in the Old Testament as a very serious offence against God. What the sin consists of can scarcely be defined in one simple formula, but broadly speaking it is a violation of JHWH's divine honour for man to dictate to him; man is demonstrating his suspicion and *unbelief* in not regarding JHWH as trustworthy, reliable, faithful to the covenant (נאמן, πιστός). To test God is thus the opposite of believing in him and therefore a very definite violation of the covenant bond. According to the Old Testament JHWH reacts in anger by determining to exterminate his people.[13]

---

[13] Cf. the texts dealt with below and Sommer and Seesemann, op. cit.

The traditions of the Israelites contained a classic example of this kind of sin: the events which took place during the desert wandering at the place called simply "Temptation" (or "Testing"), Massah (מסה), which the LXX rightly translates Πειρασμός.[14] The main account is given in Ex 17. Israel, which has just been proclaimed "the first-born son of JHWH", delivered with wonders and mighty works out of its bondage in Egypt and given manna to satisfy its hunger, now begins to thirst for water and fear for its life, doubting whether God would again save his people. Moses receives God's command to cause water to spring forth from the rock, and the place is called Massah because "they put JHWH to the test by saying, 'Is JHWH among us or not?'" (Ex 17:7).

The basic principle is here revealed. The test is designed to find out *whether "JHWH is among us or not"*. Another point that deserves notice is that the sin is accentuated because JHWH *has already* given proofs to his covenant son of his divine power and his faithfulness to the covenant bond. In Numbers 14:22 we hear that Israel tempted JHWH in the wilderness many times, not only in Massah: JHWH speaks with indignation of "the men *who have seen my glory and my signs which I wrought* in Egypt and in the wilderness, and yet have put me to the test ten times[15] and have not hearkened to my voice ..."

In Psalm 95:6 ff it is said of JHWH "for he is our God and we are the people of his pasture ..."; then comes the warning "Harden not your hearts as at Meribah, as on the day at Massah in the wilderness, when your fathers tested me (נסוני) and put me to the proof (בחנוני) *though they had seen my work*".

Psalm 78 also helps us: Israel is spoken of as a generation, whose spirit was not steadfast (נאמנה) with God. V 11 ff speaks of how the Israelites soon *forgot the mighty works* that JHWH had done in the sight of their forefathers in Egypt and in the wilderness: dividing the seas, leading them in the daytime with a cloud, and all the night with a fiery light, and bringing streams from the rocks. "Yet they sinned still more against him ... they tested God in their heart by demanding the food they craved ... Therefore, when JHWH heard he was full of wrath; a fire was kindled against Jacob, his anger mounted against Israel; because they had no faith (האמינו, ἐπίστευσαν) in God, and did not trust (בטחו, ἤλπισαν) his saving power", v 17 ff. Further on in the

---

[14] See Korn, op. cit., p. 33 ff.
[15] The rabbinic idea that God tempted Israel "ten times" in the wilderness, and that Israel tempted God "ten times", comes from this verse. Cf. e.g. M Ab 5:4, b Ar 15 ab, ARN 34.

same psalm it says "How often they rebelled against him in the wilderness and grieved him in the desert! They tested him again and again, and provoked the Holy One of Israel. *They did not keep in mind (the saving works of) his hand*, the day when he redeemed them from the foe; when he wrought his signs in Egypt, and his miracles in the fields of Zoan" (vv 40—43).

Ps 106:6 ff also sings of the early history of the people, how when JHWH had saved them from their enemies at the Red Sea, "Then they believed (ויאמינו; καὶ ἐπίστευσαν) his words; they sang his praise. But they soon *forgot his works*; they did not wait for his counsel. They had a wanton craving in the wilderness, and put God to the test (וינסו אל; καὶ ἐπείρασαν τὸν θεόν) in the desert".

Biblical passages such as these illustrated the command in Deut 6:16 "You shall not put JHWH your God to the test, as you tested him at Massah".

We must now consider another passage which throws light upon our subject, and which is important because in it the Israelite king, the Anointed One, is acting on behalf of his people—reminding us that there was a covenant not only between JHWH and Israel but also between JHWH and the anointed king (and the royal house). In Isaiah 7 we hear how Rezin, king of Aram, and Pekah, the northern Israelite king, are approaching Jerusalem to besiege it. The court was in dismay: "When the house of David was told ... his heart and the heart of his people shook as the trees of the forest shake before the wind", v 2. The prophet Isaiah receives from JHWH an oracle, a divine assurance that the enemies will not succeed but will instead themselves be judged. Judah is here exhorted to demonstrate its covenant faith (i.e. in this case, to trust that its covenant God will deliver it): "if you will not believe (תאמינו), surely you shall not be established (תאמנו)", v 9.[16] Ahaz receives permission from JHWH to ask a sign (שאל לך אות), but he refuses with the words "I will not put JHWH to the test (אנסה)", v 12. Then JHWH himself promises to give a sign to the house of David: "Behold, a young woman shall conceive and bear a son, and shall call his name Immanuel (עמנו אל)—*God with us*", v 14. Here too the basic question is "*Is JHWH with us or not?*"; but here JHWH freely chooses to grant a proof-sign.[17]

The prohibition against putting God to the test reveals an important

---

[16] Cf. on this passage Pedersen, op. cit. 3—4, p. 417.

[17] On the meaning of "the divine presence" of W. J. Phythian-Adams, The People and the Presence (1942) and J. Abelson, The Immanence of God in Rabbinical Literature (1912). See further infra, Chap. 3 C.

element in the Old Testament conception of JHWH's covenant relation with his people. The reciprocal promises and obligations do not have to be balanced out and accounted for; indeed, the concept of *God's* covenant obligations is in the last resort an irrational one, loosing itself eventually in the inscrutability of the all-holy, sovereign God. The acts of JHWH can never be questioned, his way of fulfilling his covenant "obligations" is in the end above human criticism; man simply has to accept his division of good and evil in trust and obedience; knowing that God is "righteous" and does not forsake "the righteous man". This aspect becomes more strongly emphasised with the passage of time and the development is evident within the Old Testament. The Book of Job discusses the problem and stresses that man cannot pass judgement upon his Creator.[18] The development continues in the late Jewish period (see below Chap 4 B) and both Jesus and the early church contribute towards it. Yet the essential characteristics are present in the Old Testament writings, including Deuteronomy[19]; the covenant son will bow before JHWH in love, trust and obedience, regarding him not as a capricious god of fate, but as a loving Father who, while he can chastise his son with much severity, will never permanently reject him.

D. *Other implications of the temptation theme*

In many of the Old Testament writings which the Jews loved and revered, diligently read and frequently quoted, God tempts his elect ones to test their character and inquire into their way of life. It is apparent from these passages that temptation was not *originally* regarded as an educative act;[20] according to the *basic* idea its aim is not to train, nor even to discipline or punish, but simply to find out about the person's real attitude to God, what he is "in his heart", beneath his exterior.

As we have already seen however, the idea soon came to have other implications. As more emphasis was laid on the divine omniscience, so the God who tries the heart and reins and knows all about man in his inmost self[21] is not felt to need to institute special acts of inquiry

---

[18] See further Pedersen, Israel 1—2, p. 283 ff. (cf. 3—4, pp. 401—506 passim) and Engnell, art. Jobs bok, in Sv. Bibl. Uppslagsv. 1.

[19] Cf. Pedersen, op. cit. 3—4, p. 482 ff., and R. Sander, Furcht und Liebe im palästinischen Judentum (BWANT 4. F., 16. H., 1935), pp. 3—12.

[20] Cf. Sommer, op. cit., p. 8, and Seesemann, art. cit., p. 25 f.

[21] See Ps 7:10; 17:3; 26:2; 139; 1 Sam 16:7; Jer 11:20; 17:10; 20:12; 1 Chron 29:17; Prov 15:11; 16:2; 21:2; 24:12 etc.

to learn about his creatures.[22] There were also other and more important reasons why the temptation theme was broadened and enriched. The covenant relationship was seen in terms of the father-son relationship, and so it became natural to regard temptation as the paternal act of discipline and a part of the son's upbringing. The development in this direction began early; it can be traced in the Old Testament and not only in its youngest parts. The verb נסה is sometimes placed in parallelism with בחן, "to test by trial",[23] or צרף, "to test by fire", "purge",[24] and found with verbs like יסר, חוכיח and ענה, "to mortify", "to discipline", "to bring up".[25]

Since the covenant relationship is defined in family terms these aspects are naturally taken up into the picture. In the Book of Proverbs there are many sayings from the ancient patriarchal pedagogic about the hard discipline which a man has to impose on his son.[26] Israel's heavenly father would work by the same principles. Prov 3:12 is well known "JHWH reproves (יוכיח) him whom he loves, as a father the son in whom he delights".[27] In Ps 11:5 there occurs another saying, often quoted by the rabbis, "JHWH tests the righteous; but his soul hates the wicked and him that loves violence".[27a] In Ps 94:12 the man is pronounced blessed whom God chastens and teaches (תיסרנו ··· תלמדנו); cf also 119:71. Other examples could be named.[28]

A theme often presented and extended in the inter-testamental literature is that it is *the son's privilege* to receive discipline and temptation from God, for that shows that he is not rejected but remains in a

---

[22] Cf. passages in previous note.

[23] Ps 26:2; 95:9; Wis 2:17, 19; 3:5 f.; 11:9 f.; 1 QH 2:14. Cf. also Sommer, op. cit., p. 12.

[24] Ps 26:2. Cf. further Ps 11:3; 17:3 ff.; 66:10; Jer 9:6; Zach 13:9; Prov 17:3; 27:21.

[25] E.g. in Deut 8, see infra.

[26] E.g. Prov 19:18 ff.; 29:17.

[27] So MT; but the LXX has clearly preserved the true text in this case "and he punishes (μαστιγοῖ = ויכאב) the son in whom he delights". The parallelism requires a verb in this line. The וכאב (MT) is presumably the result of a midrashic interpretation. The influence of the Son of God theme is here very apparent.

[27a] Because of its content I translate as the rabbis. Many modern translators take ורשע with צדיק. So also RSV.

[28] Interesting parallels between what is said about the king (or the royal house) in 2 Sam 7:14 f.; Ps 89:27 ff. etc, and what is said about the people of God make it probable that on this point too there was a traditional complex of symbols, originally applicable to the king in his cultic sufferings. On the problem see I. Engnell, The 'Ebed Jahve Songs and the Suffering Messiah in "Deutero-Isaiah", in Bull. of the J. Ryl. Libr. 31 (1948), pp. 54—93, and Ahlström, op. cit. in toto.

filial relationship to him. This is true of Israel as a people, and of every righteous member of it: Sir 2:1, Wis 3: 1—6, 11:9 f, 12:20—22, 2 Macc 6:12—16, 7:32 f, 10:4, Jud 8:25—27 etc.[29] Two passages in the Psalms of Solomon express the idea succinctly. The first refers to the people Israel "Thy (JHWH's) discipline is upon us, as upon a first-born, an only-born son" (18:4). The second refers to the righteous Israelite, "He (JHWH) warns the righteous as a beloved son, and chastens him as a first-born son" (13:9); cf also 3:4 f, 10:1—3, 11:15.

It has rightly been pointed out that there is a great difference between the Hebrew מוסר and the Greek παιδεία.[30] In cultured hellenistic circles "education" (παιδεία) meant the whole process of character training needed by a young man; it specially designated his spiritual and intellectual instruction.[31] The Hebrew מוסר meant chastening, discipline, supervision, and had little connection with the communication of information. The verb signified the practical upbringing given by parents, often with a somewhat hard hand.[32] In the LXX and the more hellenistic of the inter-testamental writings we find the meaning of the Hebrew term softened down and somewhat intellectualised by being reproduced by the Greek παιδεία, whereas correspondingly the Greek word receives from its new context a more robust and concrete shade of meaning than it has in secular usage. A slight influence, not more, from the hellenistic ideal of education can be traced in some of the inter-testamental writings.[33]

The rabbinic literature has many variations of the thought that JHWH tests, disciplines and chastens the son whom he loves, sometimes referring to the people Israel and sometimes to the individual. Ps 11:5 and Prov 3:12 are often quoted.[34] As the rabbis pondered over the problem of suffering and the hard paths into which God was calling his chosen people this theme gave comfort and encouragement.[35]

---

[29] See further Korn, ΠΕΙΡΑΣΜΟΣ, Marcus, Law in the Apocrypha, pp. 29—33, and Ziener, Die theologische Begriffssprache, pp. 99—104. Cf. also W. Wichmann, Die Leidenstheologie (BWANT, 4, H. 2, 1930) with its clearly expressed but somewhat over-argued thesis.

[30] See G. Bertram, Der Begriff der Erziehung in der griechischen Bibel, in Imago Dei (Festschr. G. Krüger, 1932, pp. 33—51).

[31] See on this W. Jaeger's magnum opus Paideia: the Ideals of Greek Culture 1—3 (1939—1945).

[32] See W. Jentsch, Urchristliches Erziehungsdenken (BFCT 45. Bd., 3. H., 1951), pp. 85—139 (with literature).

[33] Cf. Ziener, op. cit., p. 103 f.

[34] E.g. Mek. Bachodesh 10 (ed. Lauterb. vol. II, p. 272 ff.); Sifre Deut § 32 (ad 6:5); b Ber 5a.

[35] See Schechter, Some Aspects, pp. 52—56, Moore, Judaism 2, pp. 252—256,

A pun that the rabbis often used deserves mention. The verb נִסָּה means "to test, tempt" but can also mean "to exalt". In the latter case it often glides over into a homonymous verb נַשָּׂא, which also sometimes means "to exalt".[36] This double meaning causes many sentences like the following: " 'JHWH tempts the righteous'—this means that the Holy One, blessed be he, never exalts a man without first having tested and tempted him; if that man withstands the temptation, then he exalts him."[37] Abraham, Isaac and Jacob are among those to whom this is applied.

Since therefore the verb נסה (πειράζειν) is used alongside other terms for discipline and education, it is enriched by their overtones; it has something of this meaning even when it occurs in Deuteronomy.[38] In 8:2 ff, with which the accounts of Jesus' temptation are so clearly connected, the wandering in the wilderness and the feeding with manna are seen in terms of education and discipline; "And you shall remember all the way which JHWH your God has led you these forty years in the wilderness, that he might humble you and test you (למען ענתך לנסתך, LXX: ὅπως ἂν κακώσῃ σε καὶ ἐκπειράσῃ σε) to know what was in your heart, whether you would keep his commandments, or not. And he humbled you and let you hunger (ויענך וירעבך, LXX: καὶ ἐκάκωσέν σε καὶ ἐλιμαγχόνησέν σε) and fed you with manna ... that he might make you know that man does not live by bread alone, but that man lives by everything that proceeds out of the mouth of JHWH ... Know then in your heart that, as a man disciplines his son, JHWH your God disciplines you (מיסרך, LXX: παιδεύσει σε). So you shall keep the commandments of JHWH your God, by walking in his ways and by fearing him" (8:2 ff). When the theme returns in v 15 ff we find a new aspect: the temptation does not only discipline, it prepares for a future exaltation. God gave manna to Israel "that he might humble you and test you, to do you good in the end" (למען ענתך ולמען נסתך להיטבך באחריתך, LXX: ἵνα κακώσῃ σε καὶ ἐκπειράσῃ σε καὶ εὖ σε ποιήσῃ ἐπ' ἐσχάτων τῶν ἡμερῶν σου).

Since the answer of Jesus to the first question of the tempter is taken directly from this passage, we have every cause to take note of the

R. Mach, Der Zaddik in Talmud und Midrasch (1957), passim, and infra, Chap. 4 B.

[36] See Jastrow, Dictionary, sub vocibus. NB the spelling נסא.

[37] Num R 15:12; Cant R II, 16:2. See further Gen R 32:3; 34:2; 55:2—3; Ex R 2:2—3 etc. Cf. also such words as Sir 2:1.

[38] On God's paternal care for his people in Deut see also A.C. Welch, Deuteronomy, the Framework to the Code (1932), pp. 93—101.

meanings here attached to the word "tempt". The forty years of Israel's wandering are seen in the dual light of discipline and temptation. The temptation is to show what lies in the heart of the Son of God, whether he loves God and is ready to obey him in everything (cf also 13:3), and is also a part of the humiliation, discipline and education which God imposes upon his son before bestowing upon him the riches of his goodness.

Here, as in many other points, Deuteronomy spans the gap between the classical Old Testament and the late Jewish literature.

Our theme has also another aspect: temptation as *seduction*, as a lure to sin. This aspect will be dealt with later (see especially Chap 9).

CHAPTER THREE

The temptation narrative (Matt 4:1–11) and Deut 6–8

A. The introduction (v 1)

a) The text

Τότε ὁ Ἰησοῦς ἀνήχθη εἰς τὴν ἔρημον ὑπὸ τοῦ πνεύματος πειρασθῆναι ὑπὸ τοῦ διαβόλου.

(1) εἰς—διαβόλου] 4—6 1—3 7—10 א *K pc* sy.

b) The Son of God is led by the Spirit of God

We have already emphasised the connection between the baptism and temptation narratives. At his baptism Jesus receives the Spirit and is proclaimed Son of God by the heavenly voice. Then the Spirit leads him out into the place of the temptation and there Satan subjects him to the tests of divine sonship. Later we shall discuss the connection more closely (Chap 7). We shall here assume it and concentrate upon two elements: the Son of God being led by the Spirit and being tempted by Satan.

In Romans 8:14 "for all who are led (ἄγονται) by the Spirit of God are sons of God", Paul is using the words with their Christian implications; but he is expressing a thought familiar to the Old Testament and to the rabbis. It was, of course, axiomatic that "the son of God" had "the Spirit of God" and the problem is that ideas about the Spirit (רוח, πνεῦμα) in both Old Testament and late Jewish times were very changeable and their relation to the Son of God theme was by no means uncomplicated. It was a very common—though not universal—idea in late Jewish times that the Spirit of God (meaning principally *the spirit of prophecy*) had petered out with the prophet Malachi and would return again only in the future era of Salvation. Yet this idea could not erase the fundamental concept that Israel as the Son of God, as his chosen people, always has God's Spirit in its more general sense.[1]

---

[1] See Abelson, The Immanence of God, pp. 174—274, I. Abrahams, Studies in Pharisaism and the Gospels 2 (1924), pp. 120—128, A. Marmorstein, Studies in Jewish Theology (1950), pp. 122—144, and R. Meyer, art. προφήτης, in Theol. Wörterb. z. N.T. 6, pp. 813—828. In the last named article the position of the prophecy in the teaching and community life of the Qumran sect is also considered. — On the connection between *sonship* and *obedience*, see the references in Billerbeck, Komm. 1, p. 219 f.

According to the late Jewish expositors, the Spirit of God was particularly active among the people of God at the time of the exodus and wandering in the wilderness, either in a general way throughout the whole period, or localised in the pillar of fire and the pillar of cloud, or as taking possession of Moses or the elders or the whole people.

In Numbers 11:10 ff (cf Ex 18:13 ff; Deut 1:9 ff) Moses complains to JHWH about his thankless commission to "carry" (נשא) the people on behalf of JHWH "as a nurse carries the sucking child" (v 12), so JHWH causes his Spirit (רוח, πνεῦμα), which enabled Moses to "carry" the people, to descend upon the seventy elders; when the Spirit rests upon them, they begin to prophesy (v 25). Joshua in his zeal tells Moses that two of the men who were absent, Eldad and Medad, had also been filled with the Spirit and were prophesying in the camp, and asks him to forbid them; but Moses rebukes him and expresses the wish that all JHWH's people were prophets, that all were filled with the Spirit in this fullest sense (v 29).

Other Old Testament passages about the desert wandering speak of the presence and activity of the Spirit at this time. Neh 9:20 (2 Esd 19:20) tells of JHWH sending his good Spirit (רוחך הטובה, LXX: τὸ πνεῦμά σου τὸ ἀγαθόν) to instruct them, and this theme receives fuller treatment in Is 63, where the connection between sonship and the covenant is brought out. In v 8 JHWH says "Surely they are my people, sons who will not deal falsely", and the following verses tell how, in spite of his saving acts, they rebelled "and grieved his holy Spirit" (רוח קדשו, τὸ πνεῦμα τὸ ἅγιον αὐτοῦ, v 10, cf Ps 106:33) and in v 11 come the words "Then he remembered the days of old, of Moses his servant. Where is he who brought up out of the sea the shepherds of his flock? Where is he who put in the midst of them his holy Spirit?" Further on, in v 14, occur the words "like cattle that go down into the valley, the Spirit of JHWH gave them rest (תניחנו, LXX: ὡδήγησεν αὐτούς). So thou didst lead (נהגת, ἤγαγες) thy people, to make for thyself a glorious name". Then the speaker turns to JHWH and, in v 16, says "For thou art our Father (אבינו), though Abraham does not know us and Israel does not acknowledge us; thou, JHWH, art our Father, our Redeemer from of old is thy name ..."[2]

---

[2] The distinctive character of the chapter within the Trito-Isaianic section of Isaiah is much debated; see H. Odeberg, Trito-Isaiah (Isaiah 56—66), A Literary and Linguistic Analysis (LUÅ 1931, Teol. 3), pp. 272—280.—Concerning the idea of the spirit in this context, see H. Ringgren, Word and Wisdom (1947), pp. 165—171.—The connection between the formula of Is 63:14 and the temptation narrative is noted by I. Buse, The Markan Account of the Baptism of Jesus and Isaiah LXIII, in Journ. of Theol. Stud. 7 (1956), p. 74 f., and Du-

The presence of the Spirit at the time of the desert wandering is a popular motif in the targums and midrashes. It is said that all Israelites, including the babes yet in their mothers' wombs, were filled with the Spirit and conscious of their filial relationship to God, during the progress through the sea and the wilderness.[3]

When meditating on the future era of Salvation, the rabbis could make use of expressive passages in the Scriptures: "And it shall come to pass afterward, that I will pour out my spirit (את רוחי) upon all flesh" (Joel 3:1; cf also Is 44:3), "I will take away the stony heart out of your flesh, and I will give you a heart of flesh. And I will put my spirit (את רוחי) within you ..." (Ez 36:26 f; cf 11:19 f).[4]

c) Satan and temptation

We have already seen (Chap 2 B) that the Old Testament often speaks of JHWH himself tempting mankind; in post-exilic times however came the tendency to speak more carefully about God's activity and prefer the use of circumlocutions.[5] Divine actions such as tempting, chastising, punishing and destroying tend to be ascribed to Satan— even though it is seldom denied that God is behind all that is done by him. Rarely, if ever, is this tendency taken to the point of consistent dualism. In certain circles—e.g. the Qumran sect—strong dualistic features are indeed to be found, but not even here is God relieved of all responsibility for evil and the negative sides of life. JHWH is, in the last resort, behind the activity even of the "angel of darkness" (1 QS 3:15—4:26 etc).[6] Conversely, monism is characteristic of the

---

pont, L'arrière-fond biblique, p. 289.

[3] Targ Jerush ad Ex 15:2, Mek Shirata 1, 1 ff. (ed. Lauterb. II, p. 1 ff.), Ex R 23:2, Midr Teh 68, § 14, b Sota 30 b, 31 a, b Ket 7 b etc. See further infra, Chap. 7 B.

[4] Cf. Jub 1:21—25. For references, see the works mentioned supra, n. 1, and Billerbeck, Komm. 2 (1924), p. 615 ff.

[5] The temptation itself and not its agent holds the centre of the stage. Instead of saying "God tempts", they say "man is tempted" (πειραζόμενος), is "in temptation" (ἐν πειρασμῷ) etc. See e.g. 1 Macc 2:52; Sir 44:20; Jubil 19:8 ff., Test Jos 2 (cf. Hebr 11:17!). This is pointed out by Sommer (following M. Kähler), op. cit., p. 16 ff.—See further infra, Chap. 9.

[6] On the basic outlook of the Qumran texts (strong dualist tendencies within a dominant monist world-view) see G. Baumbach, Qumrân und das Johannesevangelium (AVTR 6, 1957), H. W. Huppenbauer, Der Mensch zwischen zwei Welten (ATANT 34, 1959), and idem, Belial in den Qumrantexten, in Theol. Zeitschr. 15 (1959), pp. 81—89.—On the form the temptation motif takes in this context

pharisaic-rabbinic tradition, yet it recognises certain events which, as they seem to be a contradiction of the will of God, must be ascribed to Satan. To summarize—we find in the Judaism of this period a basic religious monism, including however certain dualistic tendencies more or less accentuated in the different traditions.

The development can be illustrated with several examples.[7] Ex 4:24 ff tells how Moses, on his way back to Egypt, was met by JHWH who desired to kill him (because, said the midrash tradition, he had acceded to the demands of his father-in-law Jethro and had left his first-born son uncircumcised). In the later version of this account, which we find in Jubil 48:2 ff it is Mastema (Satan), not JHWH, who comes to Moses to kill him; according to the palestinian targum it is the Angel of Death.[8]

Another example: in the oldest account of David's sinful numbering of the people, 2 Sam 24:1 ff, it is JHWH who incites David. The later version, 1 Chron 21:1 ff, ascribes this to Satan.[9]

To come now to the temptation narratives—in Gen 22:1 ff JHWH himself tempts Abraham by commanding him to sacrifice his son. In Jubil 17:15 ff however it is Mastema who sets himself up against Abraham in a court scene like that of the introduction to the Book of Job[10] and suggests to God that Abraham be tempted. We find this speculation even in the rabbinic tradition (e.g. b Sanh 89 b).

The opening chapters of Job seem to have played an important part in establishing the idea that Satan is the instrument of God for the temptation of the righteous.[11] It is to be noted that the author of Job speaks not merely of God giving permission—רשות, ἐξουσία, to use the terminology later employed—but also of God as the origin of the tribu-

---

see principally: K. G. Kuhn, Die in Palästina gefundenen hebräischen Texte und das N.T., in Zeitschr. f. Theol. u. Kirche 47 (1950), esp. pp. 197—211, idem, Jesus in Gethsemane, in Evang. Theol. 12 (1952—53), esp. pp. 274—285, and idem, New Light on Temptation, Sin, and Flesh in the N.T., in The Scrolls and the N.T. (ed. K. Stendahl, 1957), pp. 94—113.—Kuhn seems to overemphasize the dualistic element and hence the Iranian influence on the religious thought of the Qumran community.

[7] Cf. B. Reicke, art. Satan, in Sv. Bibl. Uppslagsv. 2 (2 uppl. 1963), W. Foerster, art. Σατανᾶς κτλ., in Theol. Wörterb. z. N.T. 7 (1961 ff.), p. 151 ff.

[8] Cf. G. Vermes, Baptism and Jewish Exegesis, in New. Test. Stud. 4 (1957—58), p. 308 ff.

[9] Cf. Dupont, op. cit., p. 289.

[10] Cf. B. Noack, Satanás und Sotería (1948), p. 41.

[11] Cf. e.g. the role played by the Book of Job in rabbinic discussion on man's duty to thank God for good and for evil, Sifre Deut § 32 (ad 6:5). See infra, Chap. 4 B.

lation, not only in the dialogues (3:1—42:6) but also in the final chapter which is directly linked to the introductory narrative in chapters 1—2; 42:11 speaks of the evil that *God* had brought upon Job.

d) Summary

Having outlined the principal features of the background, we now summarize the contents of the introductory verse, at the same time adding some further comments.

As we shall shortly notice, only the first temptation takes place in the wilderness—and therefore we must see the introduction as bearing particularly upon it. The background is the passage in Deut 8:2 ff where it is said that JHWH has led (הוליך, ἤγαγεν) Israel in the wilderness for forty years to humble and test them. A variation of this idea is—as we have already mentioned—that JHWH led his people through his holy Spirit. So in the Gospels, Jesus, the Son of God, is led out (ἀνήχθη) into the wilderness by the Spirit there to be tested just as Israel was tested.

Much discussion has centred on the significance of the wilderness (ἔρημος) in this narrative. Interpretations have ranged from the traditional home of demons, to the most appropriate place for communion with God.[12] It is quite possible that many different motifs could have influenced the narrator. Yet we must be prepared to find the main clue in Deut 8:2 f because of its connection with the first temptation, the one which takes place in the wilderness. Ἡ ἔρημος is meant to be *the place for a humiliating and testing hunger*, i.e. the conditions required for Satan's first temptation.

The temptation narrative tells of God putting his son to the test; it is God's will that is being done. This is signified in two ways: firstly, it is the Spirit of God which leads Jesus into the place of temptation, secondly, he is taken there to be tempted (πειρασθῆναι); the final infinitive indicating that this is the (divinely) determined end of the process. What happens is not an unforeseen attack on the part of the enemy: it is part of the divine plan of salvation.[13]

The temptations are carried out by Satan; but he acts simply as the

---

[12] E.g. P. Bonnard, La signification du désert selon le N.T., in Hommage et Reconnaissance ... à K. Barth (CTAP, Hors sér. 2, 1946), p. 11 ff. and W. Schmauch, In der Wüste, in In memoriam E. Lohmeyer (1951), p. 213 ff., with literature, and the commentaries. Cf. also E. Lohmeyer, Die Versuchung Jesu, in Zeitschr. f. Syst. Theol. 14 (1937), pp. (619—650) 619 ff.

[13] Cf. e.g. Fascher, Jesus und der Satan, p. 31 f.

instrument of God. This is true even of the third temptation; a similar one occurs in Deut 13:2 ff where God is expressly stated to be the cause of it (see below D).

The narrative was formed within a strongly monist world of thought. Its basic material is a product of the main Old Testament and pharisaic outlook. The writings of Pharisees and rabbis give us —significantly enough—closer parallels to what is written here than the Dead Sea Scrolls with their stronger tendencies towards dualism.

B. ¶ *The first temptation (vv 2—4)*

a) The text

Καὶ νηστεύσας ἡμέρας τεσσεράκοντα καὶ τεσσεράκοντα νύκτας ὕστερον ἐπείνασεν. (3) καὶ προσελθὼν ὁ πειράζων εἶπεν αὐτῷ· εἰ υἱὸς εἶ τοῦ θεοῦ, εἰπὲ ἵνα οἱ λίθοι οὗτοι ἄρτοι γένωνται. (4) ὁ δὲ ἀποκριθεὶς εἶπεν· γέγραπται· οὐκ ἐπ' ἄρτῳ μόνῳ ζήσεται ὁ ἄνθρωπος, ἀλλ' ἐπὶ παντὶ ῥήματι ἐκπορευ-ομένῳ διὰ στόματος θεοῦ.

(2) κ. τ. νύκτας] om. λ pc syᶜ Ir (cf par). (4) ἐπί] ἐν **CD** al. ἐκπορ.—στόματος om. **D** abg Cl.

b) Forty days and forty nights as a period of fasting

The Matthean account tells us that the first temptation takes place after Jesus has fasted in the wilderness for forty days and forty nights. Mark and Luke have another version: Jesus is tempted during a period of forty days.

Much discussion has been devoted to the origin, meaning and function of the number forty in this narrative. Forty is one of the most used of the many "symbolic round numbers" of Judaism.[14] There is a firm basis from which we can begin to answer these questions.[15] The number here is taken from Deut 8:2, which introduces the words quoted by Jesus in answer to the devil: "You shall remember (זכרת) all the way which JHWH your God has led you these forty years in the wilderness, that he might humble you and test you ... and he humbled you and let you hunger ..." (v 2 f).

We recall that the verb ענה (pi'el) not only has the general meaning "to humble" but also the special meaning "to humble (oneself) by

---

[14] See W. H. Roscher, Die Zahl 40 im Glauben, Brauch und Schrifttum der Semiten (1909) and—esp. for late Judaism—J. Bergmann, Die runden und hyperbolischen Zahlen in der Agada, in Monatschr. f. Gesch. u. Wiss. d. Judent. 82 (1938), p. 370 ff.

[15] Cf. Meyer, Die evangelischen Berichte, p. 445 ff.

fasting".[16] The expositors could take the verb in this sense, since in v 3 it is parallel to רעב, "to hunger". They could read here not only that JHWH caused Israel to hunger (וירעבך, hiph'il) but also that he caused Israel to fast (ויענך, pi'el).

According to the early Christian narrator Jesus "remembers" (see above) what God had taught his people during the desert wandering, and he meets the tempter's suggestion with a quotation from precisely that passage in Deuteronomy (8:3). One fact seems indisputable: Jesus' forty days in the wilderness corresponds to Israel's forty years.[17] Can we go beyond this? Why is it forty *days* (and nights)?

Forty years is not the only span of time mentioned in the wilderness passages of the Old Testament; we find also mention of forty days (and nights). Moses was on the mountain fasting for just such a period before he met God (Ex 24:18, 34:28, Deut 9:9, 18). More important is the discovery that in the Pentateuch texts forty days and forty years can be corresponding periods:[18] in Num 14 the *forty years* in the wilderness are seen as a period of penance for Israel's grumbling when they were *forty days* spying out the land of Canaan, "According to the number of the days in which you spied out the land, forty days, for every day a year (יום לשנה יום לשנה), you shall bear your inquity, forty years" (14:34). If we turn to Deuteronomy we find that Moses' second visit to the mount is seen in one place (Deut 9:18) as a vicarious penance for the sins of the people; Moses says "Then I lay prostrate before JHWH as before, forty days and forty nights; I neither ate bread nor drank water, because of all the sins which you had committed, in doing what was evil in the sight of JHWH ...". Since Deut 9 is a survey of Israel's refractoriness during the period of the wilderness wandering, it is tempting to interpret Moses' penance for the sins of all the people

---

[16] Then the נפש is to be supplied. Cf. Gesenius, Lexikon sub voce. In the causative forms the נפש is not a reflexive object but an ordinary object.

[17] This seems impossible to G. Kittel: "Die vielfach hergestellte Beziehung der Erzählung zu den 40 Jahren Israels in der Wüste (Dt 8, 2) ist ohne jeden ernsthaften Anhalt. 40 Jahre sind nicht 40 Tage und Nächte; vor allem ist die Erinnerung an den Wüstenzug Israels n i c h t durch Dt 8, 2 (Versuchung und Erprobung Israels) bestimmt, sondern durch Erinnerung entweder an Israels Ungehorsam oder aber an die göttliche Heilszeit" (art. ἔρημος, in Theol. Wörterb. 2, p. 655). On the other hand J. Guillet emphasizes strongly the connection between Israel's and Jesus' time in the wilderness: Le thème de la marche au désert dans l'A. et le N.T., in Rech. de Science Rel. 36 (1949), pp. 161—181, and idem, Thèmes bibliques (Théologie 18, 1951), p. 23 f.—It is important not to over-emphasize the *typological* link; it is a question preeminently of a *midrashic* link between Deut 6—8 and the N.T. temptation narrative. See infra, Chap. 7 and also 11.

[18] NB R. Eliezer's hermeneutical rule 27: מנגד.

as a penance for the whole forty year period—in other words, to apply
here the principle that days can correspond to years. In any case, the
midrashic expositors were hardly backward in drawing this conclusion.
We would then have in this passage a parallel to Ez 4:5 f where the
prophet is commanded to symbolically "bear the punishment of the
house of Judah; forty days I assign you, a day for each year" (יום לשנה
יום לשנה).

Nevertheless we must not forget that "forty days and forty
nights" does not only occur in the context of the wilderness wandering,
i.e. Moses fasting on the mount. It also occurs in the Elijah saga: the
prophet goes through the desert to Horeb, the mount of God, and goes
"forty days and forty nights" without food, after having been fed by
the angel of JHWH, 1 Kings 19:8. As two such beloved figures as
Moses and Elijah were said in the Scriptures to have lived without
(earthly) food for forty days and nights in the wilderness, a fast of this
length must have been a well known motif in later Jewish tradition.[19]
Therefore we ought not to draw too definite conclusions at this point:
it would be unwise to assume that here we have a Moses—or even an
Elijah—typology.[20] As we have seen already, Jesus corresponds here
not with Moses but with *Israel*.

We conclude: the number forty is certainly taken from Deut 8:2.
Since the object of the temptation is an individual and not a people,
it is natural for the period to be forty days instead of forty years.[21]
It is however important to note that the passages concerning the wilderness wandering contain the idea that forty years and days can
correspond. It would be too far-fetched to maintain that Jesus' fast
had any vicarious atoning significance; the fast has no meaning beyond
that of the first temptation. When Matthew, in contrast to Mark and
Luke, speaks of "forty days *and forty nights*" it is not Moses-typology
but merely a set phrase from the traditional vocabulary of fasting.

c) Hunger and craving in the wilderness

In recent decades it has become very general to interpret the first
temptation in the light of the rabbinic idea that the "last deliverer"
(the Messiah) would be like the first deliverer, Moses, and so would

---

[19] Cf. Adam and Eve's fast for 40 days (Vit. Adae 6 and 14), how R. Sadoq
fasts for 40 years for Jerusalem (b Git 56a), how different rabbis "sit in 40
fasts" (b Bab Mez 33a, 85a), etc.
[20] Cf. Dupont, L'arrière-fond biblique, p. 295 ff.
[21] So rightly Meyer, p. 447.

cause manna to fall down from heaven for the people of God.[22] The reasons for this are insufficient, and it leads to an incorrect interpretation of the first temptation.

First and foremost, proper attention should be given to the messianic title involved; Jesus is not tempted as "deliverer" (גּוֹאֵל, σωτήρ) but as "Son of God"; this is not merely a question of nomenclature. He is here the typological equivalent to Israel, God's son, not to Moses, the deliverer. Furthermore, it is clear that what is being tested is not his relationship to mankind, the hungry people of God, but his relationship to God. If we consider the very varied Old Testament and late Jewish ideas about the bringer of manna and the nature of manna itself, we soon realize that it is not a question of the deliverer's hunger and how it should be satisfied; it is always presupposed that the Saviour's own needs are provided for (he stands in such a relation to God that he already has, or can expect, some kind of heavenly food). Furthermore, the traditions about the expected manna of the messianic age all make it clear that manna is *bread from heaven*. If the Messiah was to change stones into bread, it would certainly be a feeding-miracle, but it could hardly be thought of as a manna-miracle. These observations show that we would not be justified in trying to interpret the synoptic account of Jesus' first temptation in the light of the late Jewish ideas about the final deliverer as a bringer of manna.[23]

It is important that we keep strictly to the wording of the text. It is the *Son of God* who is tempted, and the scene is sketched with simple, concrete strokes. After fasting for forty days and forty nights, the Son of God is *hungry*—this is the situation which gives rise to the first temptation. Satan appears and invites him to make himself food to satisfy his hunger; the lack of food is to be overcome by the Son of God changing some stones into bread. What is the nature of the sin which Satan is inviting the Son of God to commit?

In the exegetical debate much attention has been devoted to the miracle which Jesus is invited to perform. The temptation is thought to lie in a misuse of the messianic powers (to perform a "Schauwunder" or use the powers for selfish ends etc).[24] This can scarcely be correct. There are no onlookers in the narrative—the Son of God is alone in the

---

[22] Thus Lohmeyer among others, Die Versuchung, p. 628 ff. For instances of the final deliverer dispensing manna, see Billerbeck, Komm. 2 (1924), p. 481 f.

[23] See additional note 2, Bread from the earth and bread from heaven.

[24] On this interpretation (Eitrem, Fridrichsen, Lohmeyer, Bultmann & others) see e.g. R. Bultmann, Die Geschichte der synoptischen Tradition (4 ed. 1958), p. 271 ff. with Erg.-heft (1958), p. 38 f.

wilderness. Neither the miracle itself nor its nature receive any emphasis. The setting of the incident is not just a picturesque backcloth lacking any real connection with the actual dialogue; it is in fact a deliberate introduction to the subject of the first temptation. The Son of God, alone in the wilderness, is hungry after fasting for forty days. Satan invites him to get bread by performing a miracle; but Jesus replies with a scriptural quotation that man should not live by bread alone but by all that which proceeds from the mouth of God. The main problem here cannot be when, where and how miracles are to be performed. Our attention should be directed instead to the Old Testament and late Jewish ideas about *hunger and its satisfying,* above all in the forms in which these appear in the texts dealing with the wilderness period. (See additional note 2: Bread from the earth and bread from heaven.)

It is fundamental for the Old Testament that God, as the creator and sustainer, gives life and food to all that he has created. JHWH "gives food to all flesh" (נותן לחם לכל בשר), Ps 136:25; he "gives food to the hungry", Ps 146:7. Ps 104 (cf especially v 27 f; also Ps 145:15) expands this theme extensively. The Old Testament emphasises that the chosen people of JHWH, God's covenant sons, his pious ones, can feel secure from threatened hunger. "The young lions suffer want and hunger; but those who seek JHWH lack no good thing", Ps 34:10; "Behold, the eye of JHWH is on those who fear him, on those who hope in his steadfast love, that he may deliver their soul from death and keep them alive in famine", Ps 33:18 f; "In the days of famine they have abundance", Ps 37:19. Job 5:17—23 describes how JHWH can reprove and chasten his chosen one, yet nevertheless will finally deliver him "for he wounds, but he binds up; he smites, but his hands heal ... in famine he will redeem you from death, and in war from the power of the sword."

These are not accidental figurative phrases; this is a fundamental element in the faith of the Old Testament and the late Jewish world. The blessing (ברכה) which JHWH promises to his people includes everything that is necessary for real living: life, health, vitality, fertility; provisions of all kinds; protection from hunger, sickness, attacks of wild beasts, human enemies, demons, etc, Deut 28:1—14 etc.[25]

According to Deuteronomy and other texts of the Old Testament Israel enjoyed this "blessing" to the fullest degree during the wilderness period. It is stated concisely in Deut 2:7, "these forty years JHWH your God has been with you; you have lacked nothing"; and Neh 9:21, "Forty years didst thou sustain them in the wilderness and they lacked

---

[25] Cf. supra, Chap. 2 A, and infra, Chap. 3 C b.

nothing". For obvious reasons the rabbis combined these sentences with the more general description in Ps 23:1, how JHWH looks after his flock, "The Lord is my shepherd, I shall not want".[26]

The desert wandering passages stress however that JHWH so arranged the feeding of his people that it was at the same time a temptation. What they received was not earthly food, or, to use the Hebrew word which has important associations in this context, earthly "bread" (לחם; Deut 29:5, Num 21:5). It can therefore sometimes be said that they were hungry (Deut 8:2 f etc). Then God gave them food from heaven, manna (Ex 16, Deut 8 etc).[27] It is related however that Israel was discontented with this divine food and complained about the manna, "this worthless food" (Num 21:5, 11:6). They *were filled with a strong craving* (התאוו תאוה, LXX: ἐπεθύμησαν ἐπιθυμίαν), a longing for the fleshpots of Egypt (Ex 16:2 f, Num 11:4 ff, 21:4 ff), they murmured and grumbled and nagged, wanted another kind of food, quails (Ex 16, Num 11). According to the texts it was with reluctance and anger that JHWH gave this food to his people (Num 11:10, 33 f, Ps 78:26 ff). The rabbis said that the manna was given by God with a light countenance, but the quails with a dark.[28]

Israel's discontent with the food that JHWH was miraculously giving them was a kind of craving (AV "lust"): תאוה, ἐπιθυμία (Num 11:4 f, Ps 78:18, 29 f, 106:14 f, Wis 16:2, 19:11). One of the stopping places owed its name to the people's craving for quails, which had resulted in the death of many of them: Kibroth-hattaavah (קברות התאוה, Μνήματα τῆς ἐπιθυμίας), "graves of craving", Num 11:33 f, Deut 9:22 etc. This indicates the clear and marked place which Israel's craving had in the traditions of the wilderness period. The Pauline midrash in 1 Cor 10:1 ff bears further witness to this.

The sin of craving in the wilderness is also elucidated in Ps 78:18 ff:

"They tested God in their heart
   by demanding the food they craved (לנפשם).
They spoke against God, saying,
   'Can God spread a table in the wilderness?

---

[26] Midr Teh 23, § 3. Israel received all that it wished in the desert, ibid. See also Ex R 21:10, 25:3 etc.

[27] God's pedagogical purpose in the wandering and the episode of the manna was discussed by the rabbis. See Mek Beshallach 1, 57 ff. (ed. Lauterb. I, p. 173 f.). The idea is present even in Deut (8:2 f.!). Cf. also Ex 16:4 where the perspective is much narrower.

[28] Mek Vayassa 3, 52 ff. (ed. Lauterb. II, p. 105).

He smote the rock so that water gushed out
 and streams overflowed.
Can he also give bread,
 or provide meat for his people?' "[29]

To satisfy one's own hunger was never regarded as a sin within the
genuine Old Testament tradition: on the contrary, to do so was proper
and natural. A strong hunger meant that the "heart" was languishing
away, "my heart is smitten like grass, and withered, because I forget
to eat my bread" (Ps 102:4). Hunger meant that life was passing away
(Num 11:6 etc). It was therefore good and in accordance with God's
will, that man should satisfy his hunger or, to use an expressive Hebrew phrase, should "strengthen one's heart with bread" (סעד לבו לחם).[30]
Hunger, like all "craving of the heart" (תאות לב), was not in itself regarded as evil or sinful. Only when hunger and eating come in conflict with
what JHWH has ordained or with the conditions he has "sent" are they
sinful.[31] The sin of the wilderness generation was that "they tempted
the Lord in their hearts by craving meat" when he had ordained otherwise.

The real nature of the sin of craving is here revealed. Discontent
with the divine nourishment provided during the wilderness period is
characterised as unbelief, lack of trust (אמונה), as a violation of the
basic obligation of the covenant. In Num 11 Moses says that the Israelites' dissatisfaction with manna means that "you have rejected JHWH
who is among you", v 20, that they thought that "JHWH's hand was
shortened", v 23. In Ps 78 it is said that the children of Israel "had no
faith in God, and did not trust his saving power", v 22; "despite his wonders they did not believe", v 32; or, in Ps 106, "then they believed his
words; they sang his praise. But they soon forgot his works; they did
not wait for his counsel", v 12 f.

---

[29] The details differ slightly in different parts of the O.T. Here in Ps. 78 the
demand for bread *before the manna is given* is dictated by sinful craving. This
does not however affect the point.

[30] For the expression, see Gen 18:5, Judges 19:5, Ps 104:15.—Cf. Judges 19:21 f.
and Acts 14:17, 2:46.

[31] Concerning "craving", "desire", cf. F. Büchsel, ἐπιθυμία κτλ., in Theol. Wörterb. z. N.T. 3 (1935—38), pp. 168—172. NB that in certain late Jewish circles
"craving", "desire" tended to be the sin par excellence. See Billerbeck, Komm.
3, pp. 234—42. On craving in the Qumran writings, see Kuhn, op. cit. (Chap 3 A
n. 6), and Murphy's op. (see below, n. 39). "Craving" as a late Jewish idea must
also be seen against the background of the notion "flesh". See Kuhn, op. cit.,
and the exhaustive article σάρξ κτλ., by E. Schweizer, F. Baumgärtel and
R. Meyer in Theol. Wörterb. z. N.T. 7, pp. 98—151, with literature.

Thus we learn that the sin for them lies not in the craving itself but in the discontent, distrust, unbelief and disobedience towards JHWH which the craving in this case signified.

d) Craving, unbelief and the divided heart

How did the late Jewish expositors regard this? How did they interpret the sin of the wilderness generation? There is not much material in the midrashes to help us answer this question. The passages narrating these occasions were not regarded as suitable for much edifying exposition. We can however get some indications by examining rabbinic opinion about desire (craving) and belief in general.

It is well known that the "heart" (לבב, לב) is used as an inclusive term for man's inner nature, not only as the "seat" of the animal instincts but also as the "seat" of faith and knowledge of God.[32] (It is necessary to place the word "seat" in quotation marks since there is hardly a question of localising these qualities to one part of the body.) Using the Old Testament terminology, the rabbis would speak of the righteous man as one who has a clean, whole and undivided, "perfect" heart (בר לבב, תם לבב or לבב שלם), as one "who seeks God with his whole heart" (דרש את יי בכל לבבו), as one "who loves God with his whole heart" (אהב את יי בכל לבבו).[33] The ideal is the integrated and uncomplicated personality wholly consecrated to the service of God. Conversely the doubter and the unbeliever is one who has "two hearts" (שני לבבות),[34] a "divided heart" (לב חלוק)[35] etc.

As Seitz has rightly pointed out,[36] the Greek translations made by the Jews show the difficulties of finding exact Greek equivalents for these expressions. The word καρδία has different connotations. Normally a righteous man, wholly devoted to God, is described as τέλειος or ἁπλοῦς (τῇ καρδίᾳ etc) while for the doubter and half-hearted such

---

[32] See F. Baumgärtel, J. Behm, καρδία κτλ., in Theol. Wörterb. z. N.T. 3, pp. 609—616. Cf. also Büchsel, art. cit., p. 169 f.

[33] Cf. in the O.T.: (a) Ps 24:4; 73:1 (b) Ps 78:72; 101:2 etc, (c) 2 Kings 20:3; Is 38:3; 1 Chron 12:39; 2 Chron 15:17 etc, (d) Deut 4:29, (e) Deut 6:5; 10:12; 13:4 etc. Note that in Deut, which delights abundant formulas, the word "soul" is drawn in to help to express total personality, "with all thy heart and all thy soul". On the command to love and fear God, cf. R. Sander, Furcht und Liebe im palästinischen Judentum, pp. 3—12 (on Deut).

[34] Midr Teh 14, § 1, Tanch תבא § 1 (ed. Buber V, 23 b § 3) etc. See infra n. 36.

[35] Sifre Deut § 32 (ad 6:5) etc.

[36] See O. Seitz, The Relationship of the Shepherd of Hermas to the Epistle of James, in Journ. of Bibl. Lit. 63 (1944), p. 134 ff., and idem, Antecedents and Signification of the Term δίψυχος, ibid. 66 (1947), p. 211 ff.

terms as διπρόσωπος, διπλοῦς and δίψυχος (cf also δίγλωσσος, Sir 5:9, ἐν καρδίᾳ δισσῇ, Sir 1:28)[37] are employed. The latter is divided and half-hearted in his worship and falls therefore a prey to craving (ἐπιθυμία, i.e. יצר הרע, תאוה etc) and temptation.[38]

In this connection we often come across the idea of the "inclination" (יצר) or the two inclinations, the evil and the good (יצר הרע and יצר טוב), which man has in his heart (לבב). The discoveries at Qumran have given us further enlightenment on this idea and it is now possible to follow its development from the Old Testament to the rabbinic literature.[39] All that is necessary here is to outline the most important variations. Sometimes there is mention of just one inclination, "the inclination of the heart" or simply "the inclination". This is good or evil depending on its conformity to the will of God. This way of thinking is found in some of the Qumran writings.[40] The rabbinic literature speaks more often—though by no means always—of *two* inclinations in the heart, the evil and the good.[41] The good inclination is good by definition; it desires the Law of God, is satisfied by it, and is perhaps nothing other than the Law of God as it functions in the heart of man. The evil inclination is not on the other hand sinful in itself; it is created by God and is necessary for the maintenance of life. Hunger, thirst, the reproductive instinct etc, are seen as legitimate expressions of the evil inclination.[42] But it is *inclined* towards evil and it leads into sin when it succeeds in bringing man to that which is contrary to the will of God. For this reason it must be restrained and disciplined (כבש, משל, שלט), brought to obey the Law. This is achieved by man listening to the word of God, by learning to "live by every word

---

[37] See C. Edlund, Das Auge der Einfalt (ASNU 19, 1952), p. 51 ff. (62).

[38] See Seitz, Antecedents, p. 212 ff.

[39] See F. C. Porter, The Yeçer Hara, in Yale Bicentennial Public., Bibl. and Sem. Stud. (1902), pp. 91—156, esp. pp. 136—156, complemented by R. E. Murphy, Yēṣer in the Qumran Literature, in Bibl. 39 (1958), pp. 334—344, esp. 342 ff., and Seitz, opera cit., also Afterthoughts on the Term "Dipsychos", in New Test. Stud. 4 (1957—58), pp. 327—334, and idem, Two Spirits in Man, ibid. 6 (1959—60), pp. 82—95.

[40] See Murphy, op. cit. Cf. also W. I. Wolverton, The Double-minded Man in the Light of Essene Psychology, in Angl. Theol. Rev. 38 (1956), pp. 166—175, and J. Licht, An Analysis of the Treatise on the two Spirits in DSD, in Script. Hieros. 4 (1958), pp. 88—100. Cf. supra, Chap. 3 A n. 6.

[41] See Porter, op. cit., S. Schechter, Some Aspects, pp. 219—292, Billerbeck, Komm. 4 (1928), pp. 466—483.

[42] On hunger and thirst as manifestations of the evil inclination see e.g. Deut R 2:33, Tanch ויגש § 1 (102 b).—Cf. Büchsel, art. cit., p. 170, and the works in the previous note.

that proceeds from the mouth of God". Then it can be said that man loves God with both his inclinations, or, that the good one reigns in his heart.[43] Sometimes it is said that the evil inclination (in its capacity of leading into sin, not in its "natural" capacity) has wholly been rooted out of the heart of a man endowed with special grace.[44]

The Old Testament does not only speak of the inclination of man's heart being evil from his youth, Gen 8:21, cf 6:5, it speaks also of the "stony heart" (לב האבן) of the sinful man, Ez 11:19, 36:26. It is not surprising that the rabbis combined these two ideas (in fact, the combination is found as early as the Qumran texts —1 QH 18:25)[45] and found a reference to the evil inclination in expounding Old Testament passages in which the word "stone" (אבן) occurred.[46] Ezekiel's prophecy of the time to come when God would remove the stony heart from his people and replace it with "a heart of flesh" and put a new spirit within them, so that they would be wholly obedient to God's statutes and ordinances (36:24 ff, 11:19 ff), was interpreted by the rabbis as referring to the evil inclination—or at least its evil functions—which would be rooted out of the heart of God's people at the coming age of salvation.[47]

Another late Jewish combination must be recorded. In Deuteronomy, as also in Jeremiah, we find references to "circumcision of the heart" (Deut 10:16, 30:6, Jer 4:4, 9:25 f). In Deut 30:6 God promises to circumcise the heart of Israel so that they will love their God with all their heart and with all their soul. These references to circumcision of the heart are found both in the Qumran[48] and in the rabbinic[49] texts, sometimes combined with references to "the inclination(s) of the heart". In the Qumran writings we also find the phrase "uncircumcision of the inclination" (עורלת יצר).[50]

These notes on the late Jewish ideas on craving (desire) must suffice. Returning now to the narrative of Israel's sinful craving in the wilder-

---

[43] The seat of the inclination is almost always the heart; Gen 6:5 and 8:21 were well-known texts! See Billerbeck, op. cit., p. 466 f., and Porter, op. cit. For the rabbinic teaching that the doctrine of the two inclinations could be deduced from the two ב in לבב and the two י in וייצר in Gen 2:7, see Billerbeck, op. cit., p. 466 f., and Porter, op. cit.

[44] See Billerbeck, op. cit., p. 479.

[45] Cf. Murphy, op. cit., p. 340.

[46] See the material in Billerbeck, op. cit., pp. 466—483 passim.

[47] E.g. b Ber 32 a, b Sukka 52 a, Ex R 41:7, Deut R 6. NB the belief that the evil inclination could be subdued by fasting, b Jom 69 b.

[48] 1 QS 5:5.

[49] E.g. b Sukka 52a.

[50] 1 QS 5:5.

ness, we can now remark in conclusion that according to late Jewish usage the sin of Israel was its divided heart towards God: its evil inclination led it into unbelief and disobedience; or, to use more general, biblical, terms: the people demonstrated that they were a "stiffhearted", a "hardhearted" people (cf חזקי לב, קשי לב in Ez 2:3,7), Ps 95:8 ff.

e) Preliminary exegesis

This extended discussion of the hunger and craving of the wilderness generation has not been a digression, for the first temptation is directly related to these themes. We quote once again the context from which Jesus takes his answer to the tempter (Deut 8:2 ff):

"And you shall remember all the way which JHWH your God has led you these forty years in the wilderness, that he might humble you and test you to know what was in your heart, whether you would keep his commandments, or not. And he humbled you and let you hunger and fed you with manna, which you did not know, nor did your fathers know; that he might make you know that *man does not live by bread alone, but that man lives by everything that proceeds out of the mouth of JHWH.* Your clothing did not wear out upon you, and your foot did not swell, these forty years. Know then in your heart that, as a man disciplines his son, JHWH your God disciplines you. So you shall keep the commandments of JHWH your God, by walking in his ways and by fearing him."

As we have already pointed out (Chap 3 A d) the wilderness in the Matthean narrative as well as in Deut 8:2 is the setting for a humiliating and testing hunger. Jesus' forty days fast was an ordinance of God of the same kind as that undergone by Israel, when the people did not get ordinary bread to satisfy them (Deut 29:5).[51] It is a test designed to discipline the Son of God and to reveal what lies in his heart. Israel did not withstand this temptation; the people were seized with craving, discontent, doubt and unbelief, and grumbled because they wanted a different kind of food to the divine sustenance God was giving them. They showed thereby that their heart was divided by craving and unbelief; the evil inclination had gained supremacy over their heart, to use the late Jewish terminology. The tempter desires to entice Jesus into this sin. Hunger is to result in a craving for earthly food, which the Son of God is to obtain for himself. But Jesus withstands

---

[51] On God's pedagogical intention with the desert wandering and the gift of manna according to Deut 8:2 f., see above, n. 27.

the temptation by "remembering" (see above) that which, according to Deuteronomy, is at hand for the Son of God. He trusts in the word proceeding from the mouth of God and rejects the temptation with it.

Some details: what does it mean that Jesus lives by that which proceeds from the mouth of God? Is it simply that he humbly and steadfastly believes in God's commandments and waits for the food which God will give him when the time of fasting is over? Or does it also mean that during this fast, a time of concentrated fellowship with God, Jesus received some kind of spiritual nourishment corresponding to Israel's manna in the desert? Both are possible, in view of late Jewish and early Christian ideas which form the background of this account (see futher below Chap 5).

It is with a stone, λίθος (אבן), or several stones, that the tempter tries to entice the Son of God into sin. The rabbis, we must remember, were notorious in the way they associated this word with the evil inclination, even when the Biblical passage scarcely justified it.[52] Is it a coincidence that the tempter here uses stones when he wants to provoke the evil inclination?[53] Or have we here an example of the way the scribal narrator strengthens his arguments by making use of a wealth of images belonging to the subject he is dealing with? The question cannot be answered decisively, for the associations are too loose to draw conclusions which will satisfy the logical minds of the West.

The stone deserves further attention however. The passages dealing with the provision of manna and of water in the wilderness both contain the idea of a miraculous *change*. It is true that in the first case, nothing earthly is changed into manna—the manna is, as already mentioned, bread from heaven—but the manna itself undergoes a miraculous change, of a positive or a negative nature (see additional note 2). With reference to the water miracle, Ps 114:8 speaks of JHWH "who turns (הפך, στρέφειν) the rock into a pool of water, the flint into a spring of water". The word of command which effects the change is a feature of the water miracle, if not of the manna. In one

---

[52] See e.g. Ex R 30:17 ad 21:18. For other examples, see Billerbeck, op. cit., pp. 466—483 passim.

[53] Luke has *one* stone (τῷ λίθῳ τούτῳ), Matt has several. According to Meyer, Die evangelischen Berichte, p. 434 ff., the singular is the original. According to Feuillet, Le récit lucanien, p. 619, the Mattean plural shows that it is not a question of satisfying Jesus' hunger but of performing a notable manna-miracle.— *If* the plural has a significance here, it could only serve—in my judgement—to underline the demand for a *superfluity* of food, a typical element in the depiction of the people's craving for sustenance.

of the accounts of how Israel complained about the lack of water (Num 20) Moses and Aaron are commanded "to tell the rock" (ודברתם אל הסלע, LXX: καὶ λαλήσατε πρὸς τὴν πέτραν, v 8)[54] to yield its water. The differences between this passage and the temptation narratives are too great for there to be any question of typological connection. Nevertheless it is interesting to note that the raw material for this presentation is also to be found in the wilderness narratives.

An important observation concerning the anthropology of the temptation narrative can be made at this point. In spite of the fact that the passage deals with hunger, craving for bread, being satisfied with the word of God etc, there is no sign of any "flesh" and "spirit" dualism.[55] This cannot be simply because the one tempted is the Son of God with special qualities and resources; it must be primarily because the narrative originated in an environment characterised by a monist outlook (that of the Old Testament and the pharisaic scribes). These verses show us how far our pericope is from the anthropology of the type found in most of the Qumran scrolls.[56]

Finally, the fundamental unity of the section on the first temptation must be noted. The subject matter is not to be found merely in the dialogue: the setting is vital to the proper understanding of the passage. The scene (the wilderness); the long fast; the hunger which tended to lead to craving, discontent and distrust; the suggestion of Satan, based on what was possible and rightful for the Son of God; all these are woven together with scribal precision into a unity based upon Deuteronomy chapter 8, as it was understood by a late Jewish scribe learned in both Scriptures and midrash.

In later chapters (5, 7 and 8) we will deal with those nuances which give the narrative its specific Christian character.

C. The second temptation (vv 5—7)

a) The text

Τότε παραλαμβάνει αὐτὸν ὁ διάβολος εἰς τὴν ἁγίαν πόλιν, καὶ ἔστησεν αὐτὸν ἐπὶ τὸ πτερύγιον τοῦ ἱεροῦ, (6) καὶ λέγει αὐτῷ· εἰ υἱὸς εἶ τοῦ θεοῦ, βάλε σεαυτὸν κάτω· γέγραπται γὰρ ὅτι τοῖς ἀγγέλοις αὐτοῦ ἐντελεῖται περὶ σοῦ

---

[54] F. Spitta refers to Job 5:23 in connection with the stone motif (Steine und Tiere in der Versuchungsgeschichte, in Zeitschr. f.d. Neutest. Wiss. 8, 1907, pp. 66—68).
[55] On "dualism" in Qumran, see supra, Chap. 3 A, n. 6.
[56] See ibid; cf. also infra, Chap. 3 E.

καὶ ἐπὶ χειρῶν ἀροῦσίν σε, μήποτε προσκόψῃς πρὸς λίθον τὸν πόδα σου.
(7) ἔφη αὐτῷ ὁ Ἰησοῦς· πάλιν γέγραπται· οὐκ ἐκπειράσεις κύριον τὸν θεόν σου.

(7) οὐκ ἐκπειρ.] οὐ πειράσεις *D*.

b) Divine protection during the wilderness wandering

Innumerable passages of the Old Testament refer to the universal *protection* granted by JHWH to his covenant son; these passages witness to varying stages in the development of the idea, but our concern here is not with this history; our interest is simply in the ideas which the late Jewish expositor could find in the sacred writings, and, for practical reasons, we will confine our attention to the protection afforded to Israel firstly during the wilderness wandering, and secondly at "the place which he had chosen", Jerusalem and its temple.

According to the Torah, God had set before his son a "blessing" and a "curse" (Deut 11:26—28, 27: 14—30:20 etc). To the blessing belonged protection from all kinds of danger: hardship, sickness, attacks of wild beasts, human enemies or demons, and all other threats to life. If Israel kept to the covenant, this protection was hers.[57]

A vivid picture of what could happen to Israel if the people forget or reject God is given in Deut 32:23 f, "I (JHWH) will heap evils upon them; I will spend my arrows upon them; they shall be wasted with hunger, and devoured with burning heat and poisonous pestilence; and I will send the teeth of beasts against them, with venom of crawling things of the dust. In the open the sword shall bereave, and in the chambers shall be terror ..." Against such threats as these the "blessing" of God is a defence and protection.

Just such a blessing rested upon Israel during the desert wandering. In Deut 8:14 ff Moses reminds the people of the wonderful protection God had given them "... JHWH your God, who brought you up out of the land of Egypt, out of the house of bondage, who led you through the great and terrible wilderness, with its fiery serpents and scorpions and thirsty ground where there was no water".

Of particular interest to us are the powerful descriptions of how JHWH as the father, protector and shepherd of his people "preserved" (שמר) and "bore" (נשא) them.

In the basic text of the covenant ritual,[58] Ex 19:4 ff, JHWH says

---

[57] See further Chap. 1 B, 2 A, D, 3 A b, B c and E b.
[58] An attempt to analyse the ritual pattern, which can be detected here, has been made by Baltzer, Das Bundesformular, but he does not deal with those elements that are of interest to us in this study.

"You have seen ... how I bore you on eagles' wings (ואשה אתכם על כנפי נשרים, LXX: καὶ ἀνέλαβον ὑμᾶς ὡσεὶ ἐπὶ πτερύγων ἀετῶν) and brought you to myself. Now therefore, if you will obey my voice and keep my covenant, you shall be my own possession among all peoples ..."

The same image occurs in Deut 32:10 ff[59] where it is said that JHWH found (ימצא) Israel "in a desert land, and in the howling waste of the wilderness; he encircled him, he cared for him, he kept him as the apple of his eye. Like an eagle that stirs up its nest, that flutters over its young, spreading out its wings (כנפיו, LXX: τὰς πτέρυγας αὐτοῦ), catching them, bearing them (ישאהו) on its pinions (על אברתו)"...

A variation of the theme appears in Deut 8:4 "your clothing did not wear out upon you, and your foot (רגלך) did not swell these forty years" (cf Neh 9:21). A similar passage is found in Deut 29:4.

It was a third variant of the theme however that was most beloved basis for late Jewish haggada. In Deut 1:31 the assurance is given that JHWH will fight for his people as "in the wilderness where you have seen how JHWH your God bore you (נשאך; the LXX has ἐτρο-φοφόρησέν σε), as a man bears his son, in all the way that you went ..." God's care for Israel in the wilderness is compared to parental care, Num 11:12 f, Is 46:3 f, Hos 11:3 and other passages.

The idea of JHWH as "father" is often combined with that of him as "shepherd", "watchman" or "protector" (שומר, רועה) of the people. These common images (Ps 23:1, 80:2, 121:3 ff etc) are also found in passages dealing with the wilderness wandering (Ps 77:21, 78:52, Is 63:11 ff—cf Ps 28:9, 79:13, 95:7, 100:3); JHWH bears his lamb etc. In Is 63:8 f we find: "in all their affliction he was afflicted and the angel of his presence saved them; in his love and in his pity he redeemed them, he lifted them up and carried them (וינשאם) all the days of old". It is not absolutely clear here whether it is JHWH or the angel of his presence who "carries" Israel through the desert.[60]

Other passages speak of JHWH "preserving" (שמר) his son Israel during the wilderness period, e.g. Josh 24:17 "and he preserved us in all the way (וישמרנו בכל הדרך), that we went." When JHWH's attendants and servants are mentioned, the protection is often executed by an angel or by a prophet: "Behold, I send an angel before you to guard you on the way "(לשמרך בדרך), Ex 23:20 (cf v 23 & 14:19, 32:34,

---

[59] On the text-critical problems of this passage, cf. Winter, Der Begriff "Söhne Gottes", p. 40 ff.

[60] On the relation between JHWH and his angel in the exodus tradition see additional note 1.

33:2). "By a prophet JHWH brought Israel up from Egypt, and by a prophet he was preserved" (נשמר), Hos 12:14.[61]

The images here reviewed were adopted and employed in the late Jewish haggadas on the wandering in the wilderness. They spoke of wild beasts not being able to harm the Israelites,[62] of the protection of angels,[63] of how JHWH carried his people as an eagle bears its young on its wings,[64] or, as man carries his son.[65] This last image, conceived in the literal manner typical of the haggadic treatment of the Biblical images, was used in many significant contexts. Even the halakists could use it. One halaka, for instance, supports its contention that a man may carry his child on his arms on the sabbath by referring to Deut 1:31, where JHWH carries Israel as a man carries his son, throughout the whole period of the wilderness wandering.[66]

c) Divine protection in the temple

Protection was, as we have already seen, one of the basic elements in the blessing which Israel enjoyed because of its covenant with JHWH. The Old Testament therefore sings not only of the protection afforded to the wilderness generation, but also of the continued, ever-present care which JHWH gives to his chosen people. *The temple* is the place par excellence where this protection is effective, for it is there that the divine presence is concentrated. We may notice here that the role played by the temple is foreshadowed in the wilderness passages, particularly in Deuteronomy. The object of all the journeyings is to reach Canaan, and in particular "the place which JHWH your God will choose" as his resting place (cf Deut 12:18, 21, 14:23 ff, 15:20, 16:2, 6, 11, 16, 17:8, 10 etc).[67]

---

[61] See previous note.

[62] See e.g. Mek Vayassa 1, 46—63 (ed. Lauterb. II, p. 87 ff.), Sifre Deut § 18 ad 1:18 f., Ex R 24:4, Num R 1:2, 21:6, 23:1, Midr Teh 22 § 11 and infra, Chap. 6.

[63] See e.g. Ex R 33:1—9, where Ps 91:11 is quoted (33:6).

[64] Mek Bachodesh 2, 18—31 (ed. Lauterb. II, p. 202 f.), Ex R 25:6, 8, 29:7, Lev R 11:3.

[65] Mek Beshallach 5, 16—36 (ed. Lauterb. I, p. 224 ff.), Mek Bachodesh 2, 31—36 (ed. L. II, p. 203), Ex R 20:2, Deut R 7:12.

[66] Num R 15:26.

[67] For instances of JHWH's protecting presence on Sion seen as a direct continuance of his presence with the people during the wilderness wandering, see Mek Pischa 14, 15—21 (ed. Lauterb. I, p. 108), Mek Beshallach 1, 172—238 (ed. L. I, p. 182 ff.) and passim.

For the Jews, Jerusalem was not only the capital city of the land; it was "the holy city"[67a], set upon "the holy mount of JHWH",[68] "the place which JHWH has chosen". It was here, they considered, that JHWH had been pleased to reside, to locate his "presence" (שכינה). In late Jewish times this saying of God about the temple was often quoted: "my eyes and my heart will be there for all time" (1 Kings 9:3, 2 Chron 7:16).[69]

The Jewish ideas about the temple were many and varied.[70] For our purposes it is necessary only to single out one element, one that is often ignored.

From ancient times, the temple was an inviolable place of sanctuary, a refuge from human enemies.[71] More than that, it also offered protection from other kinds of deadly dangers. A whole category of psalms in the Psalter[72] deal with this theme. The psalmist is in danger of his life; his "soul" (נפש) is threatened by enemies, wild beasts, plague or some other sickness, the pangs of hunger etc. He prays God to "preserve" (שמר) or "save" (e.g. הציל) him or to preserve (or save) his "soul" (נפש).[73] He says that he flees to God, "under the shadow of thy wings" (בצל כנפיך, LXX: ἐν τῇ σκιᾷ τῶν πτερύγων σου), or "under the shelter of thy wings" (בסתר כנפיך, LXX: ἐν τῇ σκέπῃ τῶν πτερύγων σου), Ps 17:8, 57:2, 61:5, 63:8 etc. These images can have a wider implication— they can, for example, refer to the general protection enjoyed by Israel

---

[67a] The formula is found in Is 48:2, 52:1, Dan 9:24.

[68] Ps 2:6; 3:5; 15:1; 24:3 etc.

[69] This oracle, originally applicable to Solomon's temple, was naturally interpreted as referring also to the *second* temple (and the temple of the future).

[70] From the wealth of literature dealing with the religious ideas about Jerusalem, Sion and the Temple, the following may be named: J. Jeremias, Golgotha (1926), p. 43 ff., R. Patai, Man and Temple (1947), M.-J. Congar, Le mystère du Temple (Lect. div. 22, 1958), W. Müller, Die heilige Stadt. Roma quadrata, himmlisches Jerusalem und Mythe vom Weltnabel (1961), pp. 179—195. For a comprehensive, though somewhat sketchy, survey of the significance of *places* in biblical thought, see W. Schmauch, Orte der Offenbarung und der Offenbarungsort im N.T. (1956).

[71] See M. Löhr, Das Asylwesen im A.T. (1930), N. M. Nicolsky, Das Asylrecht in Israel, in Zeitschr. f.d. Alttest. Wiss. 7 (1930), pp. 146—175, M. Greenberg, The Biblical Conception of Asylum, in Journ. of Bibl. Lit. 78 (1959), pp. 125—132.

[72] See I. Engnell, art. Psaltaren, in Sv. Bibl. Uppslagsv. 2 (2 ed. 1963) who, beginning with his assumption that the psalms were originally cultic poetry dealing with the ritual functions of the king (or alternatively later compositions employing motifs from the realm of sacred kingship), denotes this category "psalms of royal protection".

[73] On the formulas, see e.g. Ps 22:21; 25:20; 86:2, 13; 97:10; 121:7.

because of its covenant with JHWH—but often they expressly refer to *the temple*, e.g. Ps 36:8 f, 61:5, for it was the focus point of holiness, health and power,[74] it was where the divine "presence" was situated, where God revealed himself and took action, where the shadow of his wings was to be found,[75] the city of refuge above all others.[76]

Psalm 91 belongs to this group. Its subject is the one "who dwells in the shelter of the Most High", who "abides in the shadow of the Almighty", and who is confident of JHWH's marvellous protection, "he will cover you with his pinions (באברתו) and under his wings (תחת כנפיו) you will find refuge ..." (vv 1 and 4). The chosen one is assured of safety from "the snare of the fowler" and "the deadly pestilence", "the terror of the night" and "the arrow that flies by day", v 5. In v 11 it says "for he will give his angels charge of you to guard you in all your ways (לשמרך בכל דרכיך). On their hands they will bear you up (על כפים ישאונך), lest you dash your foot against a stone. You will tread on the lion and the adder, the young lion and the serpent you will trample underfoot".[77]

This psalm (91) contains too many images in common with the other psalms about protection in the temple for the rabbis to forget that it too was a temple psalm (see Midr Teh 91); but they also associated it with the desert wandering (Midr Teh, ibid.). This will not surprise us in view of the background we have already considered. Protection during the wilderness period and protection in the temple were portrayed with the same imagery. Innumerable associations link these two themes together, principally of course the basic theme: the covenant son is assured of protection against all dangers.[78]

---

[74] Cf. Pedersen, Israel 3—4, pp. 152—200.

[75] We do not need to deal with questions about the factual origins of this type of symbolism nor its possible connection with the cherubim, the royal throne of JHWH, in Solomon's temple; see 1 Sam 4:4; 2 Sam 6:2 ff.; 22:11; 1 Kings 8:6; 19:15; Ps 18:11; 80:2; 99:1, Is 37:14 ff. etc.

[76] We must recall a very common expression in late Jewish times. To belong to the people of God was being "under the wings of the Shekinah" (e.g. Sifre Deut § 32, ad 6:5). This very common formula shows the importance of the idea that the covenant with JHWH meant *protection*.

[77] On beasts, see infra, Chap. 6. — Ps 91 was recited in late Jewish times as a charm against demons (cf. Billerbeck, Komm. 4, p. 528 f.).

[78] There were other reasons for connecting Ps 91 with the wilderness wandering. Ps 90 is ascribed to Moses in the text and it was easy for this ascription to be held to apply to the following anonymous psalm also. See Midr Teh 90 § 4 (cf. 100 § 2), Num R 12:3.—On this question cf. H. D. Preuss, Die Psalmenüberschriften in Targum und Midrash, in Zeitschr. f.d. Alttest. Wiss. 71 (1959), p. 51 f.

d) The "wing" of the temple

Satan takes Jesus to Jerusalem and places him ἐπὶ τὸ πτερύγιον τοῦ ἱεροῦ. The meaning of this is disputed. As a building term, the word πτερύγιον (the diminutive force of the —ιον has certainly weakened) is as obscure as its synonym πτέρυξ.[79] It is possible that it is a word used for a specific part of the building, but if so it would be a rare word.

Expositors have interpreted it very differently: the tower of the temple, the temple roof, the outside edge of the roof, a projection or pinnacle, a corner of the temple building, a wing, transept or vestibule, the wall surrounding the temple area, the farthest stretch of the wall, a balcony on it, or an outwork above the outer doors of the temple.[80]

We shall suggest a possibility which could cast new light upon the whole problem. The Greek word πτερύγιον is used in the LXX twelve times out of eighteen to translate the Hebrew כנף,[81] which is also rendered by the non-diminutive πτέρυξ. As the reader will have noted, this terminology is often used in the passages dealing with divine protection (see sections b and c). It is especially significant that it occurs in Ps 91 which Satan quotes when he has led Jesus from the wilderness and placed him here. Ps 91 sings of the man whose safety lies under God's wings (תחת כנפיו, LXX: ὑπὸ τὰς πτέρυγας αὐτοῦ).

It is very probable that the narrator is using an existing —though rare—name for some place high above the ground within the temple precincts. But when he chooses such an unusual word *in this context*, he cannot be doing it unadvisedly. He knows that the word would literally mean "the wing" of the temple and he wants us to see the associations of this word. What could be a more appropriate setting for tempting the Son to misuse God's promise of protection?

Considered in isolation this theory may seem far-fetched; but in our investigation we shall try to show how the author has depicted every scene in his narrative with careful attention to detail.

e) Tempting God

In Chapter 2 C we considered the implications of the phrase "to tempt God" and only a résumé is necessary here. To understand the phrase

---

[79] See J. Jeremias, Die "Zinne" des Tempels (Mt. 4, 5; Lk. 4, 9), in Zeitschr. d. Deutsch. Paläst.-Ver. 59 (1936), pp. 195—208.

[80] See the summary of suggestions by different scholars in Jeremias, op. cit., p. 195 f., and further N. Hyldahl, Die Versuchung auf der Zinne des Tempels, in Studia Theol. 15 (1961), pp. 114—118.

[81] Jeremias, op. cit., p. 197.

we must recall the account of the temptation at Massah. The covenant son demands of God a sign to show *whether God is with him or not*, i.e. whether or not he is present and active, fulfilling his covenant obligations. This attitude is condemned in the Old Testament as one of discontent, distrust and unbelief and therefore as itself a radical breach of the covenant.

Since there are many different covenant obligations, temptation of God can take many forms. At Massah it was a test of JHWH's desire or ability to slake the thirst of his people in the desert. In the temptation narratives it is to see whether he would protect his covenant son from danger. But both are typical cases of tempting God.

Modern exegesis often associates the second temptation with the Pharisees' demand for a sign.[82] This comparison can easily sidetrack us from the real point. Firstly, there are no human onlookers named or intended in our narrative; what is being tested is the relationship between God and the Son of God, and Satan is alone with Jesus.[83] Secondly, the temptation does not consist—as we have already shown —in trying to get Jesus to doubt his divine vocation and to demand a sign of confirmation. Satan wants Jesus to *tempt God*, i.e. demand from God a token that he is going to keep his covenantal promises. This distinction may seem minute, but it is important to define the significance of our narrative with exactitude.

f) Preliminary exegesis

The second temptation must be seen against this background. The connection with Deut 6—8 and with Ps 91 is indisputable, for there are direct quotations. The significance of the temptation can now be preliminarily defined. Satan exhorts Jesus to endanger himself by his own act, so as to challenge God to save his life in accordance with the covenant promises.[84]

This section displays the same unity and consistency that we have noted in the previous one. The thought is direct and clear, and all the details help to build up the picture. The dependence on Old Testament

---

[82] Among many others we may mention Fuller, The Mission, p. 37 ff.

[83] The reply that the temple place was never deserted is valid only if the narrative were describing something that actually took place; as we have it before us, it is *a piece of midrashic teaching*.

[84] Cf. Riesenfeld's exposition of the second temptation, Le caractère messianique, pp. 59—61. The author points out here that the subject of this section is precisely the avoidance of death. See infra, Chaps 4 and 5.

texts and themes is revealed throughout; the two quotations, placed in the mouths of Satan and Jesus, are not chosen at random and every detail in the episode is eloquent of its significance. The temptation is to be about protection from mortal danger; so the participants are removed from the wilderness to the pre-eminent place of divine protection: the holy city and its centre—the temple precincts.[85] In addition, the expression "wing of the temple" must have been specially chosen. Satan enforces his invitation with a reminder, from the psalm of protection, 91, of the divine promises on which the Son of God can rely.[86] He is promised protection from all forms of deadly danger; he will be preserved and "borne" by God and by his angels.

The quotation is shortened in the Greek text of Matthew, probably because the phrase "to guard you in all your ways" in its Greek form was felt to be inappropriate to the actual situation (Jesus standing on the "wing" of the temple). If the original narrative was composed in Hebrew or Aramaic—see below, Chap 10—it would be possible that this line was not omitted; the Hebrew בכל דרכיך (cf Aram.) has a very wide meaning—"in all that you do". This detail does not however affect the exegesis of the passage.

Jesus rejects the temptation by "remembering" the commandments which God gave his covenant son according to Deut 6—8: "You shall not put JHWH your God to the test" (6:16). The quotation is from the LXX and has the 2nd person singular instead of TM's 2nd person plural; and the final phrase, "as you tested him at Massah", is omitted, no doubt because the temptation concerns protection from danger and not slaking thirst, as at Massah—even though both incidents deal with tempting God.[87]

Why is this section so dominated by the theme of danger to life? We shall answer this in full in the next chapter. At this point we would merely say that the narrator wants us to see not merely that Jesus is reluctant to tempt God, but also that *he is ready, in obedience to God, to lose his life*.[88]

---

[85] Riesenfeld emphasises the importance of the fact that the second temptation takes place in the temple court, op. cit., ibid., although he gives a different reason from ours.

[86] Cf. U. Holzmeister, Diabolus exegeta Ps 90 (91) 11 s. (Mt 4, 6; Lc 4, 10), in Verb. Dom. 22 (1942), pp. 36—40.

[87] The significance of the quotations in determining the original language of the narrative is discussed infra Chap 10. (I am quite aware of the fact that the explicit O.T. quotations in the narrative *agree with the LXX*; see K. Stendahl, The School of St. Matthew, ASNU 20, 1954, p. 88 f., and Dupont, op. cit. in toto.)

[88] The second temptation is sometimes compared with the reference to the

D. The third temptation (vv 8—10)

a) The text

Πάλιν παραλαμβάνει αὐτὸν ὁ διάβολος εἰς ὄρος ὑψηλὸν λίαν, καὶ δείκνυσιν αὐτῷ πάσας τὰς βασιλείας τοῦ κόσμου καὶ τὴν δόξαν αὐτῶν, (9) καὶ εἶπεν αὐτῷ· ταῦτά σοι πάντα δώσω, ἐὰν πεσὼν προσκυνήσῃς μοι. (10) τότε λέγει αὐτῷ ὁ Ἰησοῦς· ὕπαγε, σατανᾶ· γέγραπται γάρ· κύριον τὸν θεόν σου προσκυνήσεις καὶ αὐτῷ μόνῳ λατρεύσεις.

(10) ὕπαγε] add. ὀπίσω μου ℵ *D al.* it syᶜ Ju (cf 16:23), add. ὀπίσω σου syˢ.

b) The high mountain

Jesus rejects the third temptation with a quotation from Deut 6 (v 13), a fact which indicates that in this, as in the other temptations, an examination of the themes of Deuteronomy will give us the necessary background. There are two themes which require most attention: the scene of the temptation (the high mountain) and its subject (riches and idolatry).

In Deuteronomy we find one of the most pathetic scenes of the Old Testament: Moses stands on the top of Mount Nebo and looks out over "the Promised Land"; this, God tells him, is the land that Israel is to possess, yet he himself is not to be allowed to enter it with his people.

The most detailed version is Deut 34:1—4.[89] Moses goes up from the plain of Moab to Mount Nebo, to the top of Pisgah, opposite Jericho. There JHWH shows him the whole land, and reminds him of the promise made to his forefathers that this land would be given to their descendants; then JHWH says to him, "I have let you see it with your eyes, but you shall not go over there".

In the parallel account earlier in the book (3:27) Moses receives the following command, "Go up to the top of Pisgah, and lift up your eyes westward and northward and southward and eastward, and behold it with your eyes; for you shall not go over this Jordan". This is followed by Moses' speech to the people in which he depicts the riches awaiting

---

martyrdom of James in Hesippus (Euseb., Hist. eccl. II, 23, 11 f.). This is done most recently by Hyldahl who gives noteworthy reasons for his thesis that τὸ πτερύγιον τοῦ ἱεροῦ was used as the place of execution for those to be thrown down and stoned, op. cit., pp.113—127. This thesis is to some extent consistent with the interpretation of the second temptation given here.

[89] On the connection between the high mountain of the temptation narratives and the high mountain (Nebo) in Deut 34:1—4 see Dupont, L'arrière-fond biblique, p. 295 ff. The author demonstrates the similarity between the phraseology of the two passages.

the Israelites in Canaan and commands them (to this we must return) not to allow these riches to lead them into forgetting JHWH and worshipping other gods (Deut, chaps 6 and 8).

Much rabbinic speculation was devoted to what happened to Moses on the mountain; the text lent itself to elaboration and embroidery. For example, Moses was said to have been attacked on the mountain by Satan and was able to repel him; Moses was shown the whole world and the secrets of all ages; he received a special gift of sight enabling him to see every part of the land, even those that were hidden from view etc.[90] Deut 3:27 was especially attractive for there it says not merely that Moses should look at the land lying on the other side of the Jordan but that he should look towards *all four quarters*; thus the rabbis could interpret it as a command to look over the whole world. R. Eliezer ben Hyrkanos concluded from this passage that God gave special sight to Moses to enable him to see thus far.[91] In the Apoc Bar (Syr) there is mention of Baruch seeing all the kingdoms of the world from the top of a high mountain (76:3) and many scholars have rightly concluded that this theme has been borrowed from the Moses story.[92] This being the case, the formula in Deut 3:27 has certainly influenced this passage too.

The core of the matter however is that Deuteronomy depicts Moses on a high mountain beholding, at least, the land of Canaan and all its desirable glories.

More is implied in this "beholding" than mere oracular vision. Daube has rightly called attention to the ancient legal custom on conveying property, particularly land, from one person to another for the seller to take the buyer to some vantage point, assure him of his desire to transfer it, and let the buyer "see it", "receive it with his eyes". Daube thinks it possible that the tradition of Moses on the mountain originated in a story of JHWH *handing over* the land to the leader of the Israelites.[93] Whether or not this was the origin of the story, it is very proba-

---

[90] See principally Mek Amalek 2, 74—137 (ed. Lauterb. II, p. 153 ff.) and Sifre Deut § 228 (ad 34:1).

[91] Sifre Num § 136 (ad Deut 3:27). Cf. Mek Amalek, ibid.: Moses was enabled to see all that he wanted from the top of Pisgah. These intermediate links between Deut and the temptation narratives seem to have escaped the notice of expositors completely.

[92] So e.g. Barrett, The Holy Spirit and the Gospel Tradition (1954), p. 52. Barrett rightly rejects the common theory that the high mountain is to be compared to the mythical mount of the gods or the mountain of folk legend.

[93] D. Daube, Studies in Biblical Law (1947), pp. 24—39. Daube notes the parallel with the temptation narrative, p. 35 f. ("Satan was a good lawyer ...").

ble that the late Jewish rabbis, knowing of this custom, expounded the story in the light of it.

Although the mountain here is regarded positively, either as the place for a good view over the rich country of Canaan, or as the place where the ownership of the land could be transferred, it is worth noting that in another place in Deuteronomy high mountains are seen in a very negative light as sites of idolatrous worship. In 12:1 ff Israel is warned against following the customs of their neighbours and worshipping idols. Instead they must destroy all the Canaanite sanctuaries upon the high mountains (על ההרים הרמים, LXX: ἐπὶ τῶν ὀρέων τῶν ὑψηλῶν) and upon the hills and under every green tree. Thus the high mountain is also regarded in Deuteronomy as the scene of the false worship which Israel must avoid.

c) Riches and idolatry

In Deut 6:10 ff—immediately after the Shema—there is a parenetic section in which Israel is promised great riches in the land of which she is about to take possession, and warned against forgetting JHWH her God on account of these riches and following other gods. The riches enumerated are all of the kind later designated "mamon" (ממון; similar in both Hebrew and Aramaic—the term is not found in Biblical Hebrew), i.e. goods, property and other assets of an external nature as opposed to the body and life itself.[94]

Israel is to come into the land promised to the fathers, a land with "great and goodly cities, which you did not build, and houses full of all good things, which you did not fill, and cisterns hewn out, which you did not hew, and vineyards and olive trees, which you did not plant ...", v 10 f. Then follows the warning "take heed lest you forget (שכח) JHWH, who brought you out of the land of Egypt, out of the house of bondage. You shall fear JHWH your God; you shall serve (עבד) him and swear by his name. You shall not go after other gods ...", v 12 ff.

A parallel passage is to be found in chapter 8. Here too Israel is promised entry into a fertile country, a land in whose hills iron and copper will be found, a land that will give wealth and plenty: fine houses, large herds of cattle, much gold and silver and other good things. Here too Israel is warned against forgetting (שכח) JHWH (vv 11, 14, 17) ascribing the wealth to its own power and strength, going

---

[94] On the term, see in addition to the lexica, sub voce, Billerbeck, Komm. 1, p. 434 f.

after other gods and serving (עבד) and worshipping (השתחוה) them, v 19. Instead Israel must remember (זכר) that it is JHWH "who gives you power to get wealth" (TM: חיל; the targums have נכסין, a synonym for ממון); wealth being, as we know, one aspect of the "blessing" from JHWH.[95]

We have already noted the warning against idolatry on high mountains and hills in Chap 12:2 ff.

There is another passage in 13:2 ff worth our attention. It says that if a prophet or a dreamer should come promising signs and wonders and saying "Let us go after other gods" Israel is not to listen to him, even if the sign comes to pass, "for JHWH your God is testing (מנסה, LXX: πειράζει) you, to know whether you love JHWH your God with all your heart and with all your soul ..." We note here that a promise which is given on condition that Israel serves other gods, is designated a temptation; a temptation which the God of Israel suffers his people to undergo to test their love for him.

Deuteronomy also narrates how Israel deserted to other gods even in the desert (9:16) and how in Canaan too they forgot their God and fell into idolatry (31:20; 32:15 ff) because of the riches and good living in the land.

The episode of the Golden Calf could not be erased from the traditions even though the rabbis played down the passages dealing with it; we also remember that in Paul's midrash on the wilderness wandering in 1 Cor 10, idolatry is one of the typical sins of the wilderness generation.

It is worth noting that in Deut 32:17 idolatry and demon worship are placed together, and the same identification is made in Ps 106:37 f and in later inter-testamental literature, e.g. 1 Hen 99:7. The gods of the nations were understood in late Jewish times as idols and demons. Occasionally idolatry is explicitly compared to worship of *Satan*. In 2 Kings 21 the abominations of King Manasseh are described as uninhibited idolatry. When this came to be written up in a later—but nevertheless still pre-Christian—version, Mart Is 2:3 ff, it is said that Manasseh forgot the service of the God of his fathers and served "Satan, his angels and his powers". Satan is also here called Sammael and *Matanbuchus*(?) and is given the epithets "angel of licentiousness" and "ruler of this world". It is therefore not surprising that e.g. in Pirqe R. Eliezer 45 we find the idea that "Sammael" (i.e. Satan) was in the Golden Calf. Thus the worship of the calf could sometimes be considered as Satan-worship even in this literal sense.

---

[95] On the various aspects of the divine blessing, cf. Chap. 1 B, 2 A, D, 3 A b, B c, C b-c and E b.

d) Preliminary exegesis

Since Jesus' reply to the temptation is taken from Deut 6:13, the background of which we have just investigated, the meaning of this episode is now clear: the Son of God is here tempted to forget his God for the sake of the riches of the world and to fall into idolatry (worship of Satan).

The unity of the pericope is as impressive as the two previous ones. Since the temptation is concerned with the world's wealth and the worship of Satan, Jesus is taken up into a very high mountain (εἰς ὄρος ὑψηλὸν λίαν). Satan shows him the kingdoms of the world and their glory, and offers to give them to Jesus if he will fall down and worship him. The imagery is without doubt taken from Deuteronomy (and its expository tradition), where we find that the high mountain is not only a vantage point from which to view the riches of the world and the place for the conveyance of power and possessions, but also the traditional scene for idolatrous worship. Such agreements, point by point, are naturally not coincidences—its author was a scribe who was a master of his craft.

The devil is seen as the "ruler of this world".[96] He offers Jesus "all the kingdoms of the world and the glory of them" (πάσας τὰς βασιλείας τοῦ κόσμου καὶ τὴν δόξαν αὐτῶν). We must beware of interpreting this unconsciously in modern terms simply as the offer of the functions of government;[97] an eastern ruler was the *lord* of his kingdoms and reigned over them in honour, glory, riches and great majesty. To appreciate the nuances of the passage we must realize that Satan, in offering *the kingdoms of the world and their glory*, is offering the whole might and wealth of the earth, all that the rabbis called *"mamon"* (ממון).

Jesus rejects the temptation by "remembering" the duties of the covenant son according to Deuteronomy: never to "forget" his God for the sake of earthly riches, never to fall down and worship any idol.[98]

E. *The conclusion (v 11)*

a) The text

Τότε ἀφίησιν αὐτὸν ὁ διάβολος, καὶ ἰδοὺ ἄγγελοι προσῆλθον καὶ διηκόνουν αὐτῷ.

---

[96] Cf. how this is direct expressed in the Lukan version, Luke 4:6; see Billerbeck, Komm. 2, p. 552.

[97] Cf. Meyer, Die evangelischen Berichte, p. 463.

[98] On the words "Get thee hence, Satan", see infra, Chap 3 E c.

b) The departure of Satan and the ministry of angels

That Satan retreats from the Chosen One of God, and that the angels serve him, are both themes belonging to a rich and varying Jewish tradition.[99] A detailed analysis is not required here however since these themes play a comparatively minor role in our narrative, and the following observations must suffice.

In the Old Testament —not to speak of similar ideas throughout the ancient east—we find the belief that God's image, Son, or Chosen One, as long as he remains in this relationship, is given the lordship over creation, is served by angels, and is protected from all kinds of evil (whether evil spirits, evil men, wild beasts, sickness, or other manifestations of the powers of chaos).[1] The theme is worked out in a special way within a "dualistic" (the term is used relatively)[2] framework, as, for example, in the majority of the Qumran texts. Mankind is divided into two categories, the children of light and the children of darkness. The latter are led by the spirit of wickedness in which they walk; they are wholly captured by, and given over to, Belial, the prince of the fallen world. The former are led by the divine spirit, in which they walk, and they are protected by angels etc.[3]

The "Testament of the Twelve Patriarchs" belongs to this "dualistic" and pessimistic tradition. Half a century ago, F. Spitta[4] pointed out striking likenesses between some of the phrases in this work and the temptation narrative of the Gospels. For example, in Test Naph 8 it is said of those who do good: "the devil shall flee from you and beasts shall be afraid of you and angels shall protect you", cf also Test Iss 7, Test Benj 5—6 and elsewhere. Admittedly the Test XII as a book raises many problems which are still receiving attention from scholars;[5] yet it is clear that in its present form it is a Christian work which makes

---

[99] See e.g. E. Larsson, Christus als Vorbild (ASNU 23, 1962), pp. 115—169; Mach, Der Zaddik in Talmud und Midrasch, p. 114 ff.; W. A. Schulze, Der Heilige und die wilden Tiere, in Zeitschr. f.d. Neutest. Wiss. 46 (1955), pp. 280—283. See further Chap. 6 on the theme in Mark 1:13 (with more lit.).

[1] Cf. on what has been said above on the various aspects of blessing, Chap. 1 B, 2 A, D, 3 A b, B c, C b-c, D c.—Cf. also H. Gross, Die Weltherrschaft als religiöse Idee im A.T. (BBB 6, 1953).

[2] Cf. supra, Chap. 3 A c.

[3] E.g. 1QS 3:17—4:26. See the works referred to supra, Chap. 3 A, n. 6.

[4] Die Tiere in der Versuchungsgeschichte, in Zeitschr. f.d. Neutest. Wiss. 5 (1904), pp. 323—326, and Steine und Tiere in der Versuchungs-geschichte, ibid. 8 (1907), pp. 66—68.

[5] See the review of research in E. Larsson, Qumranlitteraturen och De tolv patriarkernas testamenten, in Sv. Exeg. Årsbok 25 (1960), pp. 109—118.

use to a large extent of Jewish material, principally from the Essene tradition to which the Qumran sect belonged. The main problem centres round the nature of the editorial work done upon the original Jewish material before Test XII received its present form. It could have been a relatively free treatment of traditional texts and ideas, or it could have been a question of certain local interpolations. We need not endeavour to determine that here.[6] On the point that here concerns us, we learn that, although the writer who gave Test XII its final shape probably was acquainted with the baptism and temptation narratives of the Gospels (cf e.g. Test Levi 18) and could have been influenced by their phraseology, when he writes of the flight of Belial from the righteous, and of the angels ministering to the righteous, he is using well-known and traditional motifs and is not influenced by the Gospels at this point.

On the other hand, the *contrast* between the temptation narrative and Test XII is most enlightening. Apart from the "dualistic" tendency in Test XII which we have already noted, expressed in the division of mankind into the obedient who are protected and the disobedient who are given over to Belial, there is also an intense pessimism about the power of evil and a strong "psychological" interest in what is *within* man. In the temptation narrative of the Gospels we breathe a different atmosphere altogether: here, as in the Old Testament and the pharisaic-rabbinic tradition, the perspective is basically "monistic". The temptations do not come from the "flesh" or "cravings" within man (see the first temptation) but from the figure of Satan, who—in spite of having power over the kingdoms of the world (see the third temptation)—is nevertheless the agent of God (cf above Chap 3 A c). When he has emerged from his tests victoriously, the Son of God bids Satan depart; then the angels come forward to minister to him. This is a different way of thinking from that which we find in the Qumran sect and its successors; the Gospel material does not come from those quarters.[7]

c) Preliminary exegesis

The temptation narrative is highly stylised and very economical in its use of words. As we have already pointed out (supra, Chap 3 A b) the

---

[6] In addition to the literature noted by Larsson, op. cit., see under my art. Patriarkernas Testamenten, in Sv. Bibl. Uppslagsv. 2 (2 ed. 1963).

[7] On the other N.T. texts, where the phraseology is more like that of the Qumran scrolls, see infra, Chap. 9.

introduction to the whole passage leads also into the first temptation. There is a similar economy at the end of the pericope. The third temptation is concluded in such a way that the whole episode is thereby summed up. The first words of Jesus' reply are the beginning of the end, "Begone, Satan". It follows naturally from this to narrate how Satan departed and the angels came to minister.

In Chap 3 D we saw that the subject of the third temptation was wealth and idolatry. It seems that this temptation was placed last for two reasons, one of which we shall give in the next chapter. The other is that rebellion and idolatry were the most extreme forms of sin, and were therefore seen as the goal of all Satan's efforts;[8] when Jesus refused these, the temptations were ended; the Son of God had demonstrated his love for and his obedience to the Father (cf JHWH's words to Abraham "now I know that you fear God ...", Gen 22:12). Satan must now depart. Matthew does not narrate any further instance of Satan personally coming to Jesus,[9] although some events are described as πειρασμοί. To this we shall return in a later chapter (9).

It has been maintained[10] that the phrase ὕπαγε, σατανᾶ[11] is a genuine saying of Jesus which has been transferred from the episode of Peter's tempting words at Caesarea Philippi (Matt 16:23 & par). This is a possible but unnecessary theory. Such a phrase could well have been uttered by Jesus in the course of his ministry on more than one occasion; but also others have certainly used it, even before Jesus. The phrase is probably a familiar formula, used in exorcisms, renunciations and on other similar occasions.

What is the significance of the angels coming and ministering (διακονεῖν) to him? A common opinion among exegetes[12] is that the angels are ministering by bringing food, the "bread of angels".[13] This

[8] On idolatry as the chief sin (a genuine O.T. theme) in later texts, see e.g. Wis 13—16, Jubil 9:4—7, 3 Macc 6:11 and Arist 134 f. Numerous other passages could be quoted.

[9] Cf. A. Schlatter, Der Evangelist Matthäus (4 ed. 1957), p. 111 f. Cf. on the other hand Fascher, Jesus und der Satan, in toto.

[10] B. M. F. van Iersel, "Der Sohn" in den synoptischen Jesusworten, p. 170 f., suggests that the words ὕπαγε, σατανᾶ are the only genuine words of Jesus in the temptation narratives.

[11] The longer phrase, ὑ. ὀπίσω μου, σ., is certainly secondary.

[12] In modern times the authority and popularity of J. Wellhausen (see idem, Das Evangelium Marci, 1903, p. 7) has helped to spread this interpretation, but it is in fact an ancient one.

[13] On the discussion about "bread of angels" in Ps 78:25 and Wis 16:20 see H. Odeberg, The Fourth Gospel (1929), p. 244 ff., and also infra, the additional note on bread of the earth and bread from heaven.

is an unnecessary limitation of the scope of the ministering, which is certainly conceived in a wider and more general sense than that. It can be connected not only with all the three tests undergone by the Son of God[14] but also with the basic motif in the narrative as a whole. Their ministry could be thought of as: giving food (first temptation); protecting (second temptation); and being the attendants of the spiritual lord of the world (third temptation). Our analysis above however would suggest that even these three aspects do not cover the whole significance of the ministering of the angels; we should remember that the narrative is about the testing of the Son of God, and that the son's love has been found complete and undivided; he has shown himself to be incorruptible and perfect: πιστός, δόκιμος, τέλειος. Now his real posi-. tion and his exalted status must be indicated; this is done by describing the flight of Satan and the approach of the heavenly ministrants. There is here an impressive unity in the narrative: the traditional concepts of the Son of God and of the temptation both demand that exaltation must follow a resisted temptation (see supra, Chaps 2 and 3). The divine pleasure resting upon the victorious son must be expressed concretely.[15] In the Gospel accounts of the temptations these themes are depicted with different nuances than before; the eschatological perspective gives the note of finality and fulfilment to the sonship of God. The Son who has now been tested has the special qualities of the new age.

To this subject we will return in Chapters 7—9.

---

[14] So rightly Meyer, Die evangelischen Berichte, p. 436.

[15] When the temptation episode was regarded as an event in Jesus' life, there had to be a modification of the exaltation theme. The actual exaltation could not take place until the completion of the full amount of suffering. But the intimation of the exaltation of the Son of God, given in the conclusion of the temptation narrative, is very significant and must not be overlooked. See further Chap. 7.

CHAPTER FOUR

The temptation narrative (M) and Deut 6: 5

A. *The problem*

The detailed analysis of the previous chapter has shown how unmistakably all three parts of the temptation narrative are linked to Deut 6—8. Of crucial significance here is the fact that this link is indisputable at the three decisive points, namely the answers which the Son of God gives to the temptations: his attitude to them is therefore based on principles taken from Deut 6—8. But another fact is also significant: it is not only the three answers which are linked to Deut 6—8; these chapters also underlie the subject-matter of the temptations and even the details of their setting.

The following question now presents itself: if all three parts of the narrative are related to Deut 6—8, is there also a connection between the narrative *as a whole* and this part of the Torah? Is there a basic theme which not only links together the three parts but also connects the whole with Deut 6—8?

When we pose such a question, we naturally think immediately of the text which "presides" over the development of the sixth and subsequent chapter of Deuteronomy, the first sentences of the famous Shema, Deut 6:4—5. These words, the beginning of the principal credal confession of the Jews, were regarded as the perfect summary of the covenant bond: Israel must know that God is one, and Israel must love him with a whole and undivided devotion. This was considered the kernel of the Torah, the principal, the "greatest" and the "most weighty" of all the commandments.[1] How was this fundamental command understood in the late Jewish period?

B. *The rabbinic exposition of Deut 6: 5*

It is hardly surprising that this crucial passage was subjected to a great deal of penetrating analysis from Jewish interpreters and expo-

---

[1] See D. Daube, The N.T. and Rabbinic Judaism (1956), pp. 63—66, 247—253, B. Gerhardsson, Memory, pp. 137—142, and idem, art. Yppersta budet, in Sv. Bibl. Uppslagsv. 2 (2 ed. 1963).

sitors. Ample proof of this can be found in the rabbinic literature: in the Mishna and Tosefta, in the tannaitic midrashes, in the Talmud and in the targums. The expositions found there are by no means pieces of academic sophistry; they are deeply thought-out and the result of much meditation over the hard lot of Israel—God's chosen son—during the centuries after Antiochus and particularly during the Hadrianic persecution. The simple faith that the Son of God would find only "blessing" and "happiness" in the external sense, had now more clearly than before given way to the belief that JHWH's ways are difficult to understand and that the Son's love for the Father can never be measured by the earthly blessings he receives. The covenant texts, not least in Deuteronomy, were interpreted in a deeper sense—if an evaluative adjective be permitted—than had been common previously. Stress was laid on the duty of the people to love and praise God for all that he sends, for that which seems evil as well as for that which seems good. Job is quoted, "Shall we receive good at the hand of God, and shall we not receive evil?" (2:10) and "JHWH gave and JHWH has taken away; blessed be the name of JHWH" (1:21). God's son must be filled with a love for God that is complete and unconditional, not one that is measured by any valuation of the gifts God gives.[2]

The rabbinic texts show that these problems had a special intensity at the time of Hadrian's persecution.[3] Various sayings of the rabbis of that period (R. Eliezer ben Hyrkanos, R. Simon ben Azzai, R. Aqiba) are preserved in, for instance, the tannaitic midrash collections Sifre Deut[4] and Mekilta.[5] We learn, however, not least from the way that R. Eliezer ben Hyrkanos, a traditionalist down to the most minute detail, handles the subject that this is not a new type of scribal exegesis, but a development within an older tradition.[6]

It was axiomatic for the late Jewish expositors that the sacred Scriptures had an inexhaustible wealth of meaning. There was a tendency in exegesis—an ancient one which was in a special way developed and remoulded by Nahum of Gimzo[7] and then by his disciple R. Aqiba

---

[2] Sifre Deut §§ 31—36 (ad 6:4 ff.), esp. § 32.

[3] Moore, Judaism 2, p. 252 ff., emphasises too strongly how these ideas are related to the Hadrianic persecution. They find expression as early as the Books of Maccabees, esp. in the pharisaic 2 Macc (Chaps 6—7).

[4] Sifre Deut ibid.

[5] Mek Bachodesh 10 (ed. Lauterb. 2, p. 276 ff.).

[6] On Eliezer's faithfulness to tradition, b Sukka 28 a, b Yoma 66 b etc. On the attitude of the maccabean martyrs, e.g. 1 Macc 1:63; 2:31—38; 2 Macc 6—7.— Cf. also the exposition in 4 Macc.

[7] See W. Bacher, Die Agada der Tannaiten 1 (2 ed. 1903), p. 57 ff.

and his school[8]—to seek in the abundant formulations of the scriptural
texts the significance that lay in every detail. We need not suppose
that those rabbis were unaware that the Scriptural authors often use
many words and metaphors to give forceful and poetic expression to
the same point;[9] what they were concerned to find were the hints lying
in the text which pointed to meanings *additional to and beyond* that
which was traditionally ascribed to it. The aim was not so much to
correct what had previously been understood, but to *supplement* it.
We must remember that no rabbi assumed that the text could only
have one meaning. The same expositor could on different occasions,
or even on the same occasion, demonstrate that a single passage had
many different things to say.[10] This is particularly true of the haggadic
exegesis, i.e. the exhortatory and didactic exposition of passages that
were not directly juridical in character; the passages in other words of
the type with which we are concerned.

The pharisaic-rabbinic exposition of Deut 6:5 is found in a concentrated form in the Mishna, Ber 9:5. The mere fact that a midrashic
section is present in the midst of the mishnaic collection of traditions
shows that we have here an older block of teaching adopted into the
Mishna during the editorial process. In the Gemara[11]—as in Sifre[12]
which was edited much earlier—we have further indications as to which
tannaites contributed to the development of this text.

The text in M Ber 9:5 reads as follows:

ואהבת את ה' אלהיך בכל לבבך ובכל נפשך ובכל מאדך.

בכל לבבך בשני יצריך ביצר טוב וביצר רע.

ובכל נפשך אפילו הוא נוטל את נפשך.

---

[8] For numerous references to literature dealing with the Jewish principles of
scriptural interpretation, see Memory, pp. 33—55.

[9] When R. Aqiba and his school exaggerated the significance of details in the
text, R. Ismael's school brought against them the sound motto, "Torah speaks
in the language of men" (דברה תורה כלשון בני אדם), Sifre Num § 112 (ad 15:31), b
Ber 31 b, etc. Aqiba did not deny this in itself, but he did deny that the language
of the Torah was as shallow as human language. On this problem see L. von
Dobschütz, Die einfache Bibelexegese der Tannaim (diss. Halle-Wittenberg
1893), p. 41; cf. also E. Starfelt, Studier i rabbinsk och urkristen skrifttolkning
(STL 17, 1959), p. 62 f.

[10] E.g. Gen R 70:8, b Sanh 34 a, Mek Bachodesh 7, 55—63 (ed. Lauterb. II,
p. 252) etc. See further Gerhardsson, The Good Samaritan, p. 26 ff.—with an
unneccessary limitation to *two* meanings.

[11] b Ber 61 b (cf. 33 b, 48 b), p Ber IX, 14 b.

[12] Sifre Deut §§ 32—33 (ed. Finkelstein, p. 54 f., Vilna ed. p. 118 f.).

ובכל מאדך בכל ממונך·

דבר אחר בכל מאדך בכל מדה ומדה שהוא מודד לך הוי מודה

לו במאד מאד·

translated:[13]

*"And you shall love JHWH your God with your whole heart and with
your whole soul and with your whole might* (Deut 6:5).

With your whole heart (thereby is meant): with both your inclinations,
with the good inclination and the evil inclination.

With your whole soul (thereby is meant): even if he takes your soul (i.e.
your life).

With your whole might (thereby is meant): with your whole property.
Another saying: *With your whole might* (is meant): for whatever measure
he measures to you, you shall bring to him an overflowing thanksgiv-
ing."

This text is also found in Sifre Deut §§ 31—32 (on 6:5) in a more
developed form which we shall make use of in our exposition. The
targums also, both Onkelos and Jerushalmi (I), witness to the general
acceptance of this interpretation of the Shema in pharisaic-rabbinism,
which was the mainstream of late Judaism. The latter targum contains
practically the whole of the exposition as found in the Mishnah.[14] It
is interesting to note that the echoes of the Shema which we have in
the Qumran texts do not reflect the same interpretation.[15]

These passages give us important clues to the mind of the pharisaic
expositors of the Shema. They were certainly not unaware that the
three elements of the command taken together signified the total
involvement of the whole man. But, as has already been indicated,
they were concerned to define the special meanings which these three
phrases of the sacred text were thought to accentuate.

Some comments:—

---

[13] The text is introduced as midrashic support for a halaka; the first words read
"Man is bound to bless (JHWH) for the evil just as one blesses (him) for the good,
for it is written ...".

[14] See the targums, in loc. I have not yet been able to check the text in the as
yet unpublished Codex Neofiti, which, according to the preliminary announ-
cement, contains the full text of the palestinian fragment targum and seems to
reproduce, to an unexpected extent, targum tradition of *pre-Christian* times.
(See Vet. Test., Suppl. Vol. 7, 1960, pp. 222—245.)

[15] See the echoes in 1 QS 9:10 ff., 1 QH 14:26 f., 15:9 ff.; the material however is
not extensive enough for us to establish positively how the sect interpreted
Deut 6:5.—NB 1 QS 9:24 ff.

i) on the rabbis' reply to the question, What is meant by the command to love JHWH your God "with your whole heart" (בכל לבבך)? The answer given in the Mishna (see above) is set within a context of speculation on the two inclinations of the heart. The undivided love of the whole heart is expressed in terms of loving with *both* inclinations. The good inclination tends, by definition, towards the love of God; the evil inclination, on the other hand, must be restrained and disciplined by the word of God before there can be complete obedience.[16] Thus we could understand the formula "(You shall love JHWH your God) with both your inclinations" to mean "(You shall ...) with the evil inclination as well as with the good one".

In the text of Sifre another dictum appears (דבר אחר בכל לבבך שלא יהיה לבך חלוק על המקום), "*With your whole heart* (thereby is meant): Your heart must not be divided (or: 'smooth') towards the Place (i.e. God)."

It is evident from what has already been said that this is virtually the same thing. The idea of the two inclinations is not—at any rate explicitly—made use of; but the point is the same. (It could not indeed be otherwise for the actual text of Deuteronomy is so unambiguous): the heart must love God undividedly, without cleavage and without hypocrisy; man is to be תם, ἁπλοῦς (see above Chap 3 B d).

ii) on the rabbis' reply to the question, What is meant by the command to love JHWH "with your whole soul" (בכל נפשך)? We must first remind ourselves that the word נפש, "soul", often needs to be translated "life". The rabbis' reply varies somewhat but is always the same in essence: "(Thereby is meant) even if he takes your soul (your life)". (It is possible that the הוא here is neutral: "even if it takes (i.e. costs) your life". The thought is the same in either case. If a pious man dies a martyr's death it is not considered a matter of blind fate but the will of God.[17]) The persecutions helped Israel to understand that they must love their God even in suffering and martyrdom.[18] God is to be loved even when he does not preserve the soul of his covenant son from death, even when he demands it from him in martyrdom. In this context the rabbis used to quote Ps 44, a psalm of the suffering of the people of

---

16 NB the rabbis' exposition of Deut 6:7, Sifre § 33!

17 See the late Jewish interpretation of passages like Ps 72:14 and 116:15 (passages from Sifre and Mek cited supra).—On the vicarious and atoning nature of martyrdom see E. Lohse, Märtyrer und Gottesknecht (FRLANT 64, 1955), esp. pp. 29—32, 64—110, with literature.

18 NB the role of the hope of resurrection in this context, 2 Macc 7:9, 11, 14, 23, 29, 36; 12:43—45; 4 Macc.

God in which its "soul" is said to lie in the dust, v 25: "for thy sake we are slain all the day long, and accounted as sheep for the slaughter". They narrated also how R. Aqiba used to ponder over how he could completely and totally fulfil the fundamental command to love God with one's whole soul, until at length it became possible for him: bound to the stake at his martyrdom, he recited his Shema until death overtook him.[19]

iii) to the rabbis' reply to the question, What is meant by the command to love JHWH your God "with your whole might" (בכל מאדך)? Both targums have here the Aramaic נכסין, while the expositions in the Mishna and Sifre have the Hebrew equivalent ממון. This shows that the pharisaic-rabbinic expositors understood the relatively rare formula in the actual Deuteronomic text מאדך to mean "your property". Both ממון and נכסין signify material assets, goods and riches, and are often contrasted with life itself or the body.[20] This distinction is—as we know—apparent also in the New Testament.[21] If "with your whole soul" is understood as "with your whole life" then "with your whole might" is taken as "with all that you have", and interpreted as a command to place all one's property and riches at God's disposal, or to be ready to abstain from them for God's sake, and to bless God for whatever amount of wealth he has granted. The traditionalist R. Eliezer ben Hyrkanos posed the question why it was necessary to have the two phrases "with your whole soul" and "with your whole might", and answered it by saying that there are men for whom life (viz. "the body", גוף) was more precious than goods (ממון, mamon) and men for whom the opposite was true; for this reason both phrases stand side by side in the Scripture.[22] The duty of thanking God according to whatever measure he measures out is worked out in the last sentence of the rabbinic quotation in an extended pun that does not require discussion here.

C. The temptation narrative (M) and Deut 6:5

To return to our narrative in Matthew, we note that the first temptation is by hunger. According to Deut 8, God sent his people into the wilderness for forty years to know what was in their heart and allowed

[19] b Ber 61 b.
[20] See Billerbeck, Komm. 1, p. 434 f.
[21] Matt 6:25 ff. & par. See infra, Chap. 5, and Billerbeck, ad loc.
[22] b Ber 61 b. In Sifre Deut § 32 (ad 6:5) the saying is ascribed to R. Eliezer ben Jacob but without doubt R. Eliezer ben Hyrkanos was the author.

them to go hungry and then fed them with heavenly food, so that they might understand that man does not live by bread alone but also by all that proceeds from the mouth of God. Similarly Jesus is tempted, after fasting for forty days, by the devil's suggestion that he obtains bread for himself. We have tried to show in our analysis of this passage that this temptation is of the same kind as Israel's in the wilderness. The Son of God is invited to give way to his desire for earthly food in the same way that Israel craved food, and to anxiety as to his means of sustenance. This is undoubtedly a prime example of what in late Jewish times was understood as letting the evil inclination dominate the heart, or, having a divided heart towards God.

Israel fell for the temptation in the wilderness: Jesus overcomes it. He rejects the tempter's suggestion by referring to the command in Deut 8:3 that man should live by what proceeds from the mouth of God, showing thereby that the word of God, and not the evil inclination, reigns in his heart. He proves that he is fulfilling the commandment, "You shall love JHWH your God *with your whole heart*".

The second temptation concerns the safety of the Son of God. The tempter urges him to test God's promise to send his angels to preserve the life of his son, to "bear" him in their hands, uninjured and unharmed; in terms of some of the many scriptural passages on this theme, he is to test God's will "to preserve his soul" (שמר נפשו) or "save his soul" (הציל נפשו), i.e. his life. The texts speak of Israel in the wilderness as being preserved against every danger; of God bearing Israel "as a man bears his son"; and, in spite of this, of Israel having doubts about God's protection.

In the mind of the narrator, Jesus' rejection of this temptation does not spring from a despair of God's protection but from a profound attitude of faith, which according to the rabbis was required in the Shema and other passages, that God's covenant Son must love God "even if God takes his life", i.e. he must not *demand* that God saves him. The implications of the second temptation are not as easy to follow as the others because only the negative reason for Jesus' answer (obedience to the commandment: "You shall not tempt JHWH your God") is explicit. There can be little doubt however that, according to the narrator, it is the positive attitude which underlies Jesus' answer. The Son of God has not set his mind on "preserving his soul" at all costs. He is ready to love God "even if God takes his soul". He does not regard the privileges of sonship as a thing to be grasped and held on to at all costs, but is ready to empty himself in the service of God. The relation between the temptation narrative and the hymn in Phil 2:5 ff will be treated later (see infra, Chaps 8 and 9).

The section on the second temptation thus demonstrates that Jesus, the Son of God, fulfils the command, "Thou shalt love JHWH your God ... *with your whole soul*".

In the third temptation Jesus is offered "all the kingdoms of the world and the glory of them". This, as we have already pointed out, is the same as what the rabbis called "mamon" (ממון) or the Aramaic synonym נכסין, in its totality. The offer is made on condition that Jesus falls down and worships Satan. This is the purest form of the temptation to abandon love for God for the sake of mamon and fall into idolatry. According to the Scriptures, the covenant son Israel had fallen for this temptation first in the wilderness and then more completely after the entry into Canaan. Jesus is tempted in the same way but resists, showing thereby that he is fulfilling the commandment, "You shall love JHWH your God ... *with your whole might* (property)".

These parallels (see further the detailed exegesis, Chap 3 sections B—D) are not just coincidental. We are near to the solution of our problem about the basic theme linking the temptation narrative to Deuteronomy, more particularly Deut 6:5. Matthew, in contrast to Luke, has retained the correct order of the three temptations, otherwise it would have been more difficult for us to detect the connection with Deut 6:5.

The connection with the text of Deut 6—8, which we have repeatedly pointed out, is unmistakable. By three direct quotations the three temptations are fast bound to Deut 6—8. The principles which determine the attitude of the Son of God are in all three cases taken from what the Law says in these three chapters. It is natural therefore that Deut 6:5 should lie behind the narrative. It would have been surprising if an early Christian narrator had depicted Jesus being tempted with three peripheral or arbitrarily chosen temptations. It is only to be expected that the temptations should be over important matters, or rather, the three most important matters. Similarily it would have been strange if the commandments followed, when the Son of God's love for God is demonstrated, had been "light" ones; his relation to God would naturally be determined by the "weightiest" command, the one that summarizes and includes all the others: Deut 6:5.

There has been much discussion whether *Heb 4:15* refers directly to the synoptic temptation narratives or whether it is a general allusion to the various trials undergone by Jesus throughout his ministry. We may remark here that the phrase sums up very succinctly the subject-matter of the Matthean narrative as we have expounded it. "Jesus, the Son of God" (v 14) is "one who in every respect has been tempted like as we are, yet without sinning": πεπειρασμένον δὲ κατὰ πάντα καθ' ὁμοιότητα χωρὶς ἁμαρτίας (v 15). We note here the epithet "Son of God" and the fact that the temptations of Jesus are not specifically messianic ones but are of the same kind as ours (the people of God), and the phrase "in every respect" (κατὰ πάντα).[23] The passage in Hebrews is a significant witness to the way in which an early Christian "author" thought of the temptations of Jesus; and we note that his thoughts follow the same lines as those of the synoptic author (M): Jesus was tempted in everything, as we are, yet he was without sin.

D. *Some conclusions*

The interpretation given above (see section C) is still preliminary. It is too early to summarize with the correct nuances the meaning of our narrative; it is necessary first to examine it in the perspective of its specifically "Jesuanic" and early Christian setting. Nevertheless we can establish certain points which are justified by the analysis already concluded.

Our narrative is woven in one piece throughout. It cannot be regarded as a secondary composition, in which separate logia have been incorporated into some specially constructed framework. The one who composed the framework also formulated the questions and selected the quotations.[24]

It can also be established that our narrator was *a scribe*, with a profound acquaintance with the implications, formulations, imagery and contents of the Old Testament texts. He did not only know the texts, he was also familiar with the expositions of them offered by the leading "rabbinical" schools from the beginning of our period. The type of exegesis with which he was familiar was not that of the Saducees,[25] or of the Essenes,[26] but of the *Pharisees*. In fact our analysis has showed that our narrator has given his narrative a well thought out structure,

---

[23] It is, by the way, not impossible that κατὰ πάντα here is an allusion to the threefold "all" (כל) in Deut 6:5.

[24] Before the story reached its written stage, it could have been remodelled and supplemented, but if so, these improvements must have been made by one who recognised its midrashic character and its relation to Deut 6:5 and Deut 6—8, since nothing foreign has been introduced; *if* such alterations were made, they were not important.

[25] It is highly unlikely that there is Saducean influence here; the undivided obedience to and dependence on God which the text speaks of does not fit what we know of the Saducee attitude. Also *angels* play their part in the narrative in two places, and this seems inconsistent with Saducean views on this point (Acts 23:8).

[26] See the analysis in Chap. 3, passim.

that he uses with confident familiarity the motifs and metaphors of Scripture and the expository tradition, that he has a clear monist outlook, and, above all, that he has depicted the Son of God being tempted on precisely the three points which pharisaic learning found emphasised in Deut 6:5. We can therefore formulate the following noteworthy conclusion: the creator of the temptation narrative must have been highly educated in the Jewish (pharisaic) learning of his time. One result of our study is the conviction that *the young Christian church numbered in its ranks more than one learned ex-pharisee of the stature of Paul.*

How many from *bet Hillel*, and even from *bet Shammai*, were converted to Jesus Christ? That there were many ex-pharisees in the early church is a known fact, stated explicitly in Acts 15:5.[27] Such passages as those we are studying however remind us that this fact must be taken much more seriously in our reconstruction of the history of the gospel tradition and of the early church.[28]

Before taking this line of thought further, we must compare the interpretation of the temptation narratives given above as a whole and in its three parts with the teaching of Jesus, as we have received it in the Gospels. This will show how Jesus of Nazareth—in his attitude of life and in the central themes of his teaching—was the dominating influence on our scribe.[29]

---

[27] The trustworthiness of this item of information is debated; see the remarks and bibliography in Memory, pp. 208—213, 245—261.

[28] Cf. Memory, pp. 245—261 [and Tradition and Transmission, pp. 22—31].

[29] [*Additional note.*] In the subsequent chapters we shall see how the three moments of the temptation narrative concern in fact three decisive themes in the synoptic tradition. In addition I shall attempt to show at which points in the synoptic gospels the threefold scheme of the Shema lies behind the account. The most important of these texts are the crucifixion narrative, Matt 27: 33—50 & par. (where the order is changed), and the Parable of the Sower, together with the genuine exposition of it, given in the synoptic tradition, Matt 13:3—9, 19—23 & par. I have analysed the two last-mentioned texts exhaustively in an article "Liknelsen om fyrahanda sädesåker och dess uttydning" in Svensk Exegetisk Årsbok 31 (1966), later to be published in English, from which I quote—in translation—the concluding section:

'The exposition of the Parable of the Sower given in the gospels has the theme "the hearers of the Word" and thus connects with the central requirement of the covenant that the people of God should (effectively) hear the Word of God, love him, and do his will. Indeed, the exposition does not merely refer to *the Shema* but is actually composed on the basis of a scribal ("pharisaic") interpretation of that crucial covenant text.

This observation gives us a new criterion with which to judge the exposition. The analysis presented above, shows that the factual contents and formal

We then have relatively clear outlines of the man who created the narrative of Jesus' temptations. He cannot be characterised more

---

finesses have been preserved most clearly in the Matthean version (even though the material here has been somewhat "academised"). The Markan version gives the impression of being a vulgarisation and the Lukan a new interpretation with concrete applications in mind.

The criterion also helps us to evaluate the parable itself and therewith the relation between the parable and its exposition. The result of our investigation is that the parable, both as regards its contents and its outer form, must have been constructed for the interpretation found in the gospels.

Some conclusions. (1) *on the traditio-historical and the synoptic problems*. We have here another example of a block of traditions being found in the purest condition in Matthew. Fine points of content and form are best understood and preserved in his version. It is possible that as the traditions underwent the "work with the Word of the Lord" of the learned college of the Matthean church, they became more sophisticated than they were originally, but this would amount to nothing more than an improvement in the true spirit and style of the material.

(2) *on the question of the unity of the gospel tradition and the characteristic outlooks of the different evangelists*. The evangelists give expression to their own opinions by the disposition of their gospels as a whole, by the framework they give to the pericopae, by changing the order of the narratives, by slightly retouching the material and sometimes by inserting small additions, usually from the Scriptures. But their respect for the material they have received, particularly for the sayings of Jesus, is very noticable, even in the actual wording. In our account, Luke is the freest. I want to lay particular stress on the observation that the temptation narrative (Q version) and the "parable chapter" (the main parts of it)—as also the crucifixion narrative—all give expression, even in details, to the same central ideal for the people of the new covenant. This shows that the Christian church *before Mark* had not only the kerygma and certain doctrinal *topoi* but also a profound synthesis, a conscious covenant ideology, in fact: a *"theology"*. I believe that this is an important door into the dark room behind the evangelists.

(3) *on the Parable of the Sower and its exposition*. The parable and the exposition fit each other as hand fits glove. If the parable—in the only form we know it—is from Jesus, then the exposition is also. If the exposition is secondary, then so is the parable—in the form we know it. (I consider that we have a genuine Jesus-tradition here, but I have not discussed, far less proved, it in this essay. Certain complementary investigations need to be made before that can be established.) The essentials of the parable and the exposition seem to me to be as follows: When God's Word (now in the form of Jesus' teaching about the kingdom of God) comes to the people of God, it makes no progress with the hardened (those characterised by the phrase that they do not "love God with their whole heart"), it is only temporarily received by the irresolute and unreliable who become apostates (those who do not "love God with their whole soul"), it is soon smothered among those who are slaves to worldliness and mamon (those who do not "love God with their whole might"—meaning

exactly than with the logion in Matt 13:52: "Therefore every scribe who hath been made a disciple to the kingdom of heaven is like unto a

---

"riches"), but it bears fruit plentifully with those who have listening ears and open hearts and therefore understand what they hear and put it into practice (those who "love God with their whole heart, with their whole soul and with their whole might" and therefore "hear God's word and do it"), i.e. the true members of the covenant, the true "sons of the kingdom".

(4) *on the parables as a genre.* Only detailed studies can determine how far the Parable of the Sower is to be equated with the other gospel parables; it is certainly wrong to regard all the parables of Jesus as of one and the same kind. But we make an important step towards understanding the nature of parables if we can get an idea of the "*fundamental-parable*" of the gospels. Our narrative is a παραβολή = מָשָׁל in the sense of an "illustrating text," the main features of which are carefully thought out with a particular explanation in view. To a certain extent it is immediately understandable because of its use of traditional metaphors, particularly those belonging to the Biblical passage in question. But the intention is clearly that the parable should be closely examined, interpreted and expounded. The imagery used predisposes an exposition which will incorporate similar themes from the Scriptures and from the established traditions. In our analysis we have found evidence for a modified form of the "hardness of heart theory", though not for it in its accentuated Markan form. The parables have a veiled meaning; they therefore give to those who *have*, and withhold from those that *have not* (an elementary knowledge of God and love for him).

(5) *on the teaching of Jesus.* If the principal contents of the "parable chapter" are historically reliable—which does not necessarily mean that all the parables and sayings in it were spoken on the same occasion—it shows that Jesus did not attempt to win great crowds to himself by a teaching designed to be *easily understood*. It was undoubtedly other elements in his preaching, in his activity as a whole, and above all in his person which attracted some to him and repelled others. The "simple" came to him not because they understood his parables but for other reasons. In the intimate fellowship of the circle gathered round Jesus, with its opportunities for conversation, questions and teaching in unveiled, clear words—this is where there could be a ready intelligibility, a wisdom which could be identical with classical simplicity.

(6) *on the theological consequences.* The "parable chapter"—as also the narrative of Jesus' temptations—emphasises the continuity between the two covenants more than the discontinuity. We see the positive connection between the true Israel in the old covenant and the true Israel in the new, between the Scriptures and the proclamation of the kingdom of God, between the learning of the scribes and Jesus (the church). Here we have a complex of ideas which deserves careful reflection and the consequences of which must be fully worked out. The relation between the teachers of Israel and Jesus cannot be adequately defined simply in terms of Law and Gospel. The early church knew not only the scribal learning which was to be counted as loss, but also the scribal learning which brought its pupil "not far from the kingdom of God". Those scribes who had come to a faith in Jesus Christ and had become "disciples of the kingdom

man that is a householder, which bringeth forth out of his treasure *things new and old.*"

---

of heaven", had cause to bring out from their storehouse not only that which was "new" but also that which was "old".'

I will return to *the crucifixion narrative* in a further article.

Made in the USA
Lexington, KY
29 July 2018